CH00664496

VAGN HOLMBOE
EXPERIENCING MUSIC

VAGN HOLMBOE

EXPERIENCING MUSIC
A Composer's Notes

Translated, Edited and Introduced by
PAUL RAPOPORT

With a Foreword by
ROBERT SIMPSON

Musicians on Music
No. 5

TOCCATA
PRESS

First published in English by Toccata Press, 1991.
© Vagn Holmboe, 1981.
Translation and Introduction © Paul Rapoport, 1991.
Most of this book first appeared as *Det Uforklarlige*,
      Gyldendal, Copenhagen, 1981.

British Library Cataloguing in Publication Data

Holmboe, Vagn
Experiencing music: a composer's notes. —
    (Musicians on music, ISSN 0264-6889; no. 5)
    1. Composition (Music)
    I. Title   II. Rapoport, Paul
    III. Det uforklarlige. *English*   IV. Series

781.6'1 MT40

ISBN 0 907689 15 9 (cased)
ISBN 0 907689 16 7 (paperback)

Typeset in 11 on 12 point Baskerville by Apex Products
Printed & bound in Great Britain by Short Run Press Ltd, Exeter

Contents

List of Illustrations

FOREWORD
Robert Simpson

Vagn Holmboe's achievement as a composer has yet to be fully known in the English-speaking world; his standing in Scandinavia is unquestioned, and the years will establish that he is a master of European significance, with a vast body of varied work in many different genres. His genius truly generates – in his music things are born and they grow. In it, continuous metamorphosis is not merely ingenuity; it is life, it is tingling proliferation. Within the clear-cut outline of his musical personality is an infinity of resource. Elements that seem similar assume myriad new shapes, flying round, about, and amongst one another like birds, and as they mingle, so they change again, constantly, organically. The sharp ear of the civilised creator of such music can hear into the finest interstices of musical material, can descry ever fresher potentialities in the flux, in the changing relation of moving things. While he is doing this, Holmboe is expressing human thoughts and feelings. He is an acute but sympathetic man; he loves to see things grow – around his house he has planted thousands of trees with his own hands, and his music, so free from sentimental pretensions, so filled with real energy, truly reflects the mind that has created its own environment. Hearing his music for the first time we may find it somehow reserved, unconcerned with common emotions; even so, we are inescapably aware of a fine heat at the heart of it, a severe yet intensely human concentration that itself is a passion far outstripping self-consciousness. Selflessly, he explores himself, and finds an exactitude of expression rare in an artist of our time. Exactitude, not mere finesse, and out of it comes humanity; in his music we hear him breathe, we feel the circulation of his blood, the beating of his heart, and the working of an unusually disciplined brain that is able to safeguard the durability of its ideas.

Holmboe is also an articulate man; he has clear thoughts about music in general, about its relation to life. Through this as well as through his music he has had a deep influence on many younger composers in his own country. He observes music as a naturalist observes animals and plants, and we find touches in his words that remind us a little of Carl Nielsen; he always illuminates the connections with life. We cannot afford to be without such an artist and thinker, and I hope this book will encourage the performance and discovery of Holmboe's impressive music in places where it has yet to be heard.

EDITOR-TRANSLATOR'S INTRODUCTION

A Note on the Essays in this Book

This book presents several essays by the outstanding Danish composer Vagn Holmboe (born in 1909), whose published writings on music are, regrettably, either hard to find or written in Danish or both. These translations constitute therefore an attempt at making his thoughts more widely available to a musical public who will, I believe, be very interested in what he has to say.

The main item in this book is *Music – the Inexplicable.* It is the most recent, having been published on its own in Danish in 1981. The title itself may seem to contain an inherent contradiction: how can someone try to write about and thus in a sense explain the inexplicable? The answer is not an easy one, and can perhaps be discovered only by reading the whole essay. In any case, more than sixty years of experience as a composer, together with extensive work in music research, criticism and teaching, lie behind Holmboe's desire to deal with some of the most basic questions concerning music. He readily admits that there are problems in trying to discuss this mercurial art which is so important to so many people. But that does not deter him from trying to shed some light on the issues; and his wide-ranging musical experiences, inquisitive mind and uncommon powers of perception enable him to clarify a considerable amount in matters which are the concern of everyone connected with music.

Music – the Inexplicable is centred on considerations of the art of music from the point of view of the composer, the performer and the listener. Within the chapters devoted to each, many questions are posed and dealt with. For example: Where do musical ideas come from? What are composers' working methods, and how much are they really aware of them? What is the role of performers, and what sort of freedom do they have in interpreting music? What do listeners do in listening to music? Do you need a musical education to understand recent music? What, essentially, is the musical experience?

Throughout the essay, Holmboe takes considerable pains not to be dogmatic. He is not even didactic, but reflective, constantly provoking thought by asking questions and, if they cannot be answered, by 'circling around' them, as he puts it. It might seem that such an approach would lead nowhere, but the results are the opposite. The reader who is also inquisitive and reflective will gain much insight from Holmboe's treatment, and this regardless of agreement or disagreement with his conclusions. There is no requirement, by the way, to be a musician in order to understand the essay, nor indeed anything else in this book: Holmboe's prose, like his music, is addressed merely to his fellow human beings, whoever and wherever they may be.

In the original Danish edition of *Music – the Inexplicable*, the footnotes were printed at the back. I have adapted them to appear in the text and have added many of my own. My remarks are always enclosed by these brackets, [ ], while unmarked footnotes are Vagn Holmboe's. It is also important to know that the references to Holmboe's own compositions, whether in the main text or in the footnotes, are merely illustrations of general points; or, as he put it in connection with his own footnotes, 'The works adduced here are included exclusively as *examples* of the particular situations that may arise with the creation of musical works'. He has in no way written a book about himself or his own music, and probably felt a natural reluctance to mention his own experiences. Nonetheless, the few he has mentioned are most appropriate and illuminating.

The short additional essays included here, which enlarge the picture of Holmboe's concerns and attitudes, are all related directly or indirectly to matters raised in *Music – the Inexplicable*. The 'Epilogue' and 'On the Experiencing of Time' are from a book written twenty years before (1961), and show that in important ways Vagn Holmboe's basic beliefs about music have stood firm, although details of focus and emphasis are different in the two books. In the second, biographical section of this introduction (p. 25) I shall have a little more to say about the book *Interlude* (*Mellemspil*), from which these two essays come.

The remaining essays do not call for much comment. The one on Carl Nielsen appeared in English, translated by Eric Ruusu-

Lecturing at the Louisiana Museum at Humlebæk in 1981 (photograph by Anne Sophie Rubæk Hansen)

nen, in the publication *Musical Denmark* in its issue No. 15, Spring 1964 (pp. 1–3). The article on Joseph Haydn appeared in *Trofasthed og tradition* (Fidelity and Tradition), a collection of ten essays edited and published by Vincens Steensen-Leth, Steensgaard, 1979 (pp. 103–105). The essay on Igor Stravinsky's *Symphony of Psalms* appeared first in the journal *Levende musik* (*Living Music*), Vol. 2, No. 10, December 1943 (pp. 319–325). Here it is abridged. The original contained some discussion of specific musical aspects of the work, including nine music examples, the better to introduce it to Danish readers. The more general remarks are what is kept in this abridgement, which appears in this form with Vagn Holmboe's approval. 'Human Responsibility and Artistic Freedom' first appeared in a book of 'Musical Self-Portraits' in 1966; and 'A Little String Trio' in a book distributed by the newspaper *Jyllands-Posten* in 1966. Full details may be found in the Acknowledgements on p. 30. These two essays, along with 'On the Experiencing of Time', have already

Composer in the making:
Holmboe in 1911, nearly two years old

been reproduced in my catalogue of Vagn Holmboe's works.[1]

There is similarly very little to say about the translating of these articles, although one thing is worth pointing out. In the Stravinsky essay Holmboe appears to jump from discussing 'technology' to discussing 'technique'. But in the original this is not a sudden shift at all, since in Danish it is possible to use the same word for both, which is what Holmboe does, enabling him to relate his remarks about the gramophone to those about Stravinsky's music quite naturally, although in English this appears to be done at best by a linguistic sleight-of-hand – sleight-of-tongue, perhaps.

[1] Paul Rapoport, *Vagn Holmboe: A Catalogue of his Music, Discography, Bibliography, Essays*, Edition Wilhelm Hansen, Copenhagen, 1979.

Holmboe at the age of 26, in the summer of 1936 at Juelsminde,
Jutland, in conversation with his pet crow, Ali

A Note on Vagn Holmboe and his Music

As this is not a book about Vagn Holmboe nor a book addressed
solely to musicians, I do not wish to go into much detail about
his life or music. Nonetheless, some biographical background
may prove useful to readers who are, justifiably, unfamiliar with
him but curious about the musical person behind these essays.

Vagn Holmboe was born on 20 December 1909 in Horsens,
in east-central Jutland, Denmark. His parents were amateur
musicians who encouraged their children to take up various arts
so long as their interests in them remained amateur as well;
nevertheless, Holmboe apparently decided early that he wanted
to become an artist of some kind. With a little experience in
several of the arts, he applied for entrance into the Royal Conservatory of Music in Copenhagen, and was admitted, in 1926,
partly because of a favourable recommendation from Carl Nielsen, with whom Holmboe otherwise had little to do personally
during the remaining five years of Nielsen's life.

For entrance to the Conservatory, Holmboe submitted a string quartet, and for graduation in 1929 he submitted another. This medium has been a lifelong passion of Holmboe's: he has written thirty string quartets, although the first ten, a few of which are incomplete, he has left unnumbered and unpublished.

At the Conservatory his main teachers were Knud Jeppesen (in music theory) and Finn Høffding (in composition). In 1930 he went to Berlin and studied briefly with the composer Ernst Toch (1887–1964). In Berlin he met Meta May Graf, a Romanian pianist (known today as a painter, photographer, and maker of stained glass mosaics), whom he married in November 1933. The marriage took place in Romania during Holmboe's stay there in 1933–34. During that time he studied and collected examples of Balkan folk music, whose essence has remained an important influence on his music to the present.

Holmboe's first important composition to be published was the Sonata for Violin and Piano No. 1 (1935), issued in 1936 by the prominent Samfundet til udgivelse af dansk musik (Society for the Publication of Danish Music). His first work to be played in public 'at a genuine concert with critics and all that'[2] was a string trio from 1931. It was first played in November 1932. By then, Holmboe had written over 75 compositions, mostly for piano, small chamber groups, and small orchestras. Today he considers very few of these compositions important.

Between 1934 and 1940 Holmboe taught music privately; the depression years afforded him little else. He also published several articles on music, mainly in *Dansk musiktidsskrift* (*Danish Music Journal*). The earliest of these that is of more than passing interest ('Music – and Aesthetics') contains a brief discussion of some contemporary composers, including the Hungarian Béla Bartók (1881–1945). Holmboe's interest in Bartók increased through his travels and studies in the Balkans. Eventually he came to share many of Bartók's attitudes towards 'non-art' or 'vernacular' music, both in itself and in its relation to composing in the Western European 'art-' or 'cultivated' music tradition.

It is clear that the vernacular musics of Holmboe's studies in the mid-1930s meant very much to him, and not merely in their

---

[2] Vagn Holmboe, 'En lille strygetrio' ('A Little String Trio'); reproduced in full on pp. 128–32

*With Ernst Toch in 1951,
in the garden of Holmboe's
home in Holte*

technical features. In an article entitled 'A Little about Modern Music', published in January 1936 in *Dansk musiktidsskrift*, the discussion of the lack of acceptance of modern music and aspects of its melody, harmony and rhythm is secondary to, for example, the mentions of 'primitive' music and the idea that it could show the way towards simplification, in the best and deepest senses, in modern European music. Holmboe's repeated concern was 'the primevally musical, the feeling of the timelessly regulated', 'the spontaneous and the regulated in music's nature' – things he felt nearly all the best music possessed, whether cultivated or other music. He also felt that much Western European music of the past few centuries was not natural, profound or free enough.

Of more technical interest are three ethnomusicological reports Holmboe published in *Dansk musiktidsskrift* in the 1930s. The article 'Romanian Folk Music' discussed the music's melodic and scalar patterns, ornamentation, rhythmic and metric tendencies, instruments, and place in Romanian society. Holmboe was impressed by the Romanians' intense, fundamental musicality as well as by some technical features: melodic severity and melodic variety, certain types of metrical irregularity and rhythmic constructions, unusual scales, and harmony that was subordinate to other musical elements. Many of these features came to play important, if distilled, roles in his own music. The section on musical ecstasy and magic in *Music – the Inexplicable* also shows that Romanian music has had a strong effect on his thinking.

The mixture of Eastern and Western influences in Romania may have been partially responsible for Holmboe's further

Holmboe at the piano with the Norwegian composer Arne Nordheim, in 1956

research into 'Arabic Musical Culture', the title of a long article dealing with the subject similarly to the way he dealt with Romanian music. At the end of the article he expressed again what he found lacking in common-practice Western European music, by comparison to Arabic:

> One can certainly hear immediately that it [...] is not a strange world one comes to [i.e., the world of Arabic music], but a world of the same *kind* as the European world; but with this not trivial difference, that while Europe over the centuries was developing its harmony and thereby simplified its melody, rhythm, and phrase-construction, it was exactly these three elements which were particularly being developed in Arabic culture.

A third article, from 1938, 'The Street Song in Copenhagen', dealt with exactly that, discussing various methodological problems such as notation, classification of songs, and treatment of variants, as well as the history and characteristics of the songs themselves and their possible relation to other folk and primitive music. Regrettably, a book on Danish street songs mentioned in this article as being planned did not materialise at that time. In fact, Holmboe's active research in vernacular musics was ended at the close of the 1930s by the Second World War and by his own increased fame and activity as a composer and teacher. But in the last few years he has returned to this subject once more, and a book by him on street songs and cries has now been published (in English).[3]

During the 1930s Holmboe wrote several compositions based on Romanian or Danish folk music. One of these, a *Romanian Suite* for piano (1937) was published by Viking in 1953. A larger and slightly later example is the Symphony No. 3, *Sinfonia rustica* (1941), based on some folk material from Jutland. But such works became rarer in Holmboe's production as he involved himself more with the abstracted essences of folk music in relation to what he perceived as his own Western and Northern European cultivated-music traditions and roles.

In July 1938 Holmboe passed an organist's examination in Copenhagen, but he never taught the organ or played it as a regular occupation. As a composer he showed almost no interest in the organ until 1972. Since then he has written several works for it, largely because of requests from organists for something from him for their instrument.

Probably the most important prize Vagn Holmboe has won among the nearly two dozen awarded him in the past fifty years is the first prize in the Royal Danish Orchestra's Scandinavian competition for an orchestral work, held in 1939. The winning work was his Symphony No. 2 (1938–39). Holmboe tells an amusing story concerning this competition. Apparently, during the early rounds of the judging, the conductor Egisto Tango, who was one of the judges, was away from Denmark. The committee of judges advanced several works to a final round; Holmboe's was not among them. But when Tango returned to Denmark, he demanded to look over all the entries and then went on to insist that while Holmboe's Symphony was far from perfect, it was certainly the best composition submitted.

The prize Holmboe won was important for both professional and personal reasons. First, it spectacularly brought his name to the attention of many people in Denmark interested in music,

---

[3] *Danish Street Cries*, Kragen ApS, Copenhagen, 1988.

many of whom had never heard of him. Newspaper articles about him, his background and his work became frequent; more students wanted to study with him; performers and institutions requested works from him; his orchestral works were taken up by the major Danish orchestras. Second, the prize money enabled Holmboe and his wife to buy land on which to build, so that they might eventually move to a congenial setting, away from the capital city, too busy and too noisy, where Holmboe often found it impossible to write music. Shortly after the German invasion in the Spring of 1940, they bought land situated in Ramløse, about thirty miles from central Copenhagen: a peaceful, sparsely populated spot in gently rolling hills, not far from a large forest, Lake Arre, and the North-western coast of Zealand, the large island that makes up east-central Denmark. Over the course of about fifteen years, the Holmboes cleared and shaped the land, planted thousands of trees and other plants, and built two dwellings. They took up permanent residence there in 1953 and have lived there since then.

In 1940 Holmboe began teaching music at the Institute for the Blind in Copenhagen, a position he kept until 1949. Also in 1940 he wrote his Wind Quintet *Notturno*, his first work to be recorded: the Wind Quintet of 1932, a well-known group in Denmark, recorded it for Danish HMV in 1947.

Immediately after *Notturno*, Holmboe wrote a cantata for a dedication at the state school in his native Horsens. This was the first of three cantatas he wrote for celebrations in Horsens, and the first of the more than one dozen cantatas he has written to date for a variety of Danish institutions and celebrations. In the 1940s these cantatas were an important source of additional income and recognition for the composer.

During the war he wrote about 35 compositions, several of which have never been performed – but ought to be. Other works from the war years were considerably delayed in getting performed. During this period Holmboe wrote his Symphony No. 4, *Sinfonia sacra* (1941, revised in 1945), which won first prize in a competition sponsored by Danish Radio and therefore gained the honour of being performed at the inaugural concert for the new Danish Radio building in September 1945. This is one of Holmboe's few overtly religious works; he wrote the simple, war-related text in Danish and had it translated into Latin, which

With the British musicologist Robert Layton in 1959

is the only language in which the words are to be sung. The influence on this work of Stravinsky's *Symphony of Psalms* is obvious but by no means negative.

From 1939 to 1948 Holmboe wrote eleven Chamber Concertos for one to three soloists with small orchestras. Since he was also writing works called Symphonies in the same period (Nos. 2 to 6 are from 1938 to 1947), and since two of the Concertos have no specified soloists – one being subtitled *Sinfonia concertante* – one might well ask whether the differences between the Symphonies and the Chamber Concertos of that time, or of the later years as well, amount to more than differences in surface format. Holmboe wrote about the distinctions, characteristically naming no composers but really referring to his own work. The following comes from an article published in 1944 in *Levende musik*, entitled 'Symphony, Concerto and Contemporary Music':

> All music in which the component instruments, so to speak, give up their individuality and adapt themselves to a larger totality where they *sound together* is *symphonic* music; just the opposite is music in which the instruments enter into outright *competition* with one another, where certain instruments step forward; such music is *concertante* music.
>
> In its essence, the symphony is therefore music that is built on synthesis, on continuity, or, to say it more fashionably, it is the line and the tension that are crucial to whether a work is symphonic or not; spontaneous contrasts must be subsidiary, if the symphonic line is not going to be covered up or broken. The concerto's essence is, however, play, play between instruments or between dynamic and timbral contrasts; any line, in the symphonic sense, is contrary to the concerto's nature.

It is important that, for Holmboe, 'symphony' and 'concerto' meant not specific forms but general principles and procedures, a point he makes explicit in the same article. The passage quoted shows some of the significant ends towards which he was directing his attention in his music in the 1940s.

The recognition which Holmboe's Fourth Symphony received began to make up for the noticeable and understandable hiatus in performances of his large works during the War. His Fifth Symphony, in fact, was first performed in June 1945, before the Fourth, and came to be more widely known, especially as a result of performances that took place in 1947, in June in Copenhagen at the festival of the International Society for Contemporary Music, and later in the year in Stockholm. Over twenty years later, the Swedish musicologist Bo Wallner described the Symphony's Swedish reviews from 1947 and noted that 'we can declare right away that Vagn Holmboe's Fifth Symphony had a reception in Stockholm more unified and more enthusiastic than any contemporary Swedish or other foreign work'.[4] He went on to imply that Holmboe's significance for Swedish music, dating from the middle- to late 1940s, may have been comparable to the earlier considerable significance in Sweden of other Danish composers, such as Niels Wilhelm Gade (1817–1890) and Carl Nielsen (1865–1931).

In 1947, too, Holmboe became a music reviewer for *Politiken*, one of the two main Copenhagen daily newspapers. In 1950 he became a teacher at the Royal Conservatory in Copenhagen. His work for *Politiken* ended in 1955 when he was named Professor in Theory and Composition at the Conservatory, a position he held until 1965. At that time he 'retired' into a busy life of full-time composing, aided by a pension and by a large annual grant renewable for life from the government's cultural foundation – a very high honour given in recognition of his services to Danish music.

Holmboe was occupied with the first three of his twenty numbered string quartets in 1949, which was also the year he wrote most of his only well-known work for solo piano, the *Suono da Bardo* (*Sound from Bardo*), a large six-movement 'symphonic suite'.

---

[4] 'Reflexioner omkring en symfoni sats' ('Reflections around a Symphony Movement'), in *Dansk musiktidsskrift*, Vol. 45, No. 7, 1969, pp. 150–60.

*Holmboe with Zoltán Kodály in front of the Louisiana Museum in Humlebæk,
Denmark, ca. 1960 (photograph by Meta May Holmboe)*

Nearly all Holmboe's works can be called 'serious', as opposed
to 'comic', 'funny' or even 'lightly humorous', but in the latter
categories lie several worthy exceptions. From the 1940s came
Den galsindede tyrk (*The Ill-tempered Turk*; 1942–44), the still-
unperformed ballet; *Lave og Jon* (*Lave and Jon*; 1946–48), an unperformed opera with some fine music to a libretto by Lis Thor-
bjørnsen; and *Tolv danske skæmteviser* (*Twelve Danish Jesting Ballads*; 1948), which contain some bright, ribald ditties using Danish
and Danish-dialect texts. From later years come *Nikke nikke nambo*
(1968), six songs for children and a variety of percussion instruments, based on some nonsense poems of the Dane Benny
Andersen; *En tosset verden* (*A Crazy World*; 1966), ten songs written
for and with the help of children; and the purely instrumental
Quartetto medico (1956) for flute, oboe, clarinet and piano, written for some physician friends, with movement indications like
'Intermedico I – Andante senza pianisticitis'.

During 1950–55 Holmboe was working for both *Politiken* and
the Conservatory. During that time he moved out to Ramløse
and thereafter had to commute to the Conservatory and back

In 1963 Holmboe and Nadia Boulanger were both members of the jury of the 'Prix de composition musicale Prince Rainier III de Monaco' in Monte Carlo

several times a week in a trip that could take several hours in one direction. Despite the many demands made on his time, he managed to complete many major works: Cantatas Nos. 8 and 9; the first four volumes of motets called *Liber canticorum*, austere *a cappella* settings of biblical Latin texts; a Fourth String Quartet and a few other chamber works; Symphonies Nos. 7 and 8; a Chamber Symphony; and the unnumbered *Sinfonia in memoriam*, commissioned by Danish Radio to be played on the tenth anniversary of the liberation of Denmark from the Germans.

In 1957 Holmboe published the only article he has written so far about his own music that goes into technical musical details. As the delegate from Denmark at the international conference of composers held in Stratford, Ontario, for a week in August 1960, Holmboe delivered a paper, 'On Form and Metamorphosis'; it is the only significant article he has published in English.[5]

The Stratford paper has certain points in common with Holmboe's book, *Mellemspil – Tre musikalske aspekter (Interlude – Three Aspects*

---

[5] In John Beckwith and Udo Kasemets (eds.), *The Modern Composer and his World*, University of Toronto Press, Toronto, 1961, pp. 134–40.

of Music), which he was probably working on at the same time. (Only two small parts of this book have been translated into English, both of them being included in the present volume.) The three 'aspects' are entitled 'In the Beginning', 'In the Extremes', and 'In the Middle'. The book represents Holmboe's attempt to set down important assumptions about music and music history and to discuss his general aesthetic position, with some attention to specific subjects such as analysis, the 'avant-garde' and metamorphosis. Quite possibly it was written to provide explicit justifications for what he stood for artistically, as a response to challenges from other and younger composers that his way of music was no longer relevant or sensible. As an indication of what Holmboe's general beliefs were at the time (most of which remain today), the book is a valuable one indeed.

In *Mellemspil* Holmboe is especially interested in discussing the contemporary musical scene. 'In the Beginning' sets the stage for that discussion by presenting his views on analysis, the experiencing of musical time and communication, and the complementary nature of emotion and intellect, of conscious choice and chance impulse, and of other apparent opposites in the composing of music. Some of this would be familiar to readers of *Music – the Inexplicable*. In his discussion of the avant-garde in *Mellemspil*, he argues for the validity of an artistic avant-garde but against two extremes in musical tendencies, extremes which became prominent in the 1950s, namely, predetermined composition and aleatoric composition.[6] In both he finds an abandonment of what he considers fundamental responsibilities for a creative artist: to obey the basic laws of the art, to create an artistic whole out of potential chaos, and to communicate artistic truths (however complex or indescribable they may be) to the receivers of the artistic experience.

The section of *Mellemspil* entitled 'In the Middle' again deals with some items also discussed in *Music – the Inexplicable* (although from different perspectives), e.g., the importance of 'how' and 'why' certain musical means are used (as opposed to the lesser

---

[6] The former uses highly organised pre-arranged patterns of notes; the latter uses chance or randomising procedures in composition or performance. Both involve practices which are not usual in the Western tradition, and both may produce results which the composer cannot control or predict in the usual way.

importance of the means themselves), the significance of musical tradition and the creative forces within that tradition, and the necessity of understanding the independence of the finished work of art. In this part of *Mellemspil* he also discusses metamorphosis, a compositional procedure with which he was involved from about the late 1940s to the early 1970s:

> Metamorphosis is based on a process of development that transforms one matter into another, without it losing its identity, its basic characteristics. Metamorphic music is thus by its nature marked by unity, which among other things mean that contrasts, however strong they may be, are always made of the same material substance, and that contrasts can indeed be complementary but not dualistic.

Further explanation of metamorphosis would take us rather far afield. Let it be sufficient to note that this quotation suggests that Holmboe's music was dealing with issues which were very closely related to his concerns in *Mellemspil*, and indeed to concerns of artists and also scientists everywhere.

Mellemspil is a book which is as carefully constructed as Holmboe's music. There would have been ample justification for calling it a 'symphonic book' in three movements plus an epilogue. For that matter, *Music – the Inexplicable* is really 'Symphonic Book No. 2', for it too has subtleties of construction and form which are very important and an artistic totality in the sense Holmboe means when he writes about music. Some of this he very likely realised when he gave the chapter headings in this essay the word 'sats', used in Danish to mean 'movement', in the sense of a numbered movement of a musical composition.

Almost contemporary with *Mellemspil* is Holmboe's only performed stage work, *Kniven* (*The Knife*), a symbolic chamber opera to his own libretto about the relationship of the avant-garde to established ways. Other works of the middle and late 1950s and early 1960s include a Chamber Concerto (No. 13); String Quartets Nos. 5 and 6; three cantatas; and several choral works, including the first of three *a cappella* works Holmboe has written to Faroese texts. The other important compositions from 1955 to 1963 include string and brass quintets (one each), two solo Sonatas (for flute and for double-bass), three orchestral *Symphonic Metamorphoses*, and a series of four *Sinfonias* for string orchestra

Holmboe in 1975 with the Swedish composer Hilding Rosenberg at Rosenberg's summer residence in Skåne, Sweden (photograph by Meta May Holmboe)

which may be played separately, or as a group in an unusual interlocking form.

The years 1963 and 1964 were taken up mainly with the *Requiem for Nietzsche* (the title is spelt the same in Danish and English), a setting for tenor, baritone, chorus and full orchestra of *Nietzsche*, a set of eleven sonnets by the well-known Danish poet Thorkild Bjørnvig. The sonnets make vivid use of specific events from Nietzsche's life to create a kind of symbolic paraphrase of it – his expectations, aspirations, discoveries, conflicts and magnificent decline. Bjørnvig himself suggested later what may have interested Holmboe philosophically in the *Nietzsche* poems:[7] the struggle to maintain one's convictions and maintain and develop higher orders of artistic totalities and truths in a time of disruption, confusion, even disaster and despair. The combination of the sonnets' dispassionate formal control with their stark imagery and networks of allusions might also have attracted Holmboe, for these features, or their musical counterparts, are certainly characteristic of his music.

Since the time of his retirement from teaching in 1965, Holmboe has, as I have said, remained a very active composer. He travels infrequently, sometimes for a holiday after a period of especially intense work, sometimes to hear the first performance of a composition. His normal routine is to work on composition only from early morning to lunchtime, since other matters tend to take up the rest of his day. Some works are written quickly, some are not. For the largest works he usually writes some

---

[7] 'Ord og musik' ('Words and Music'), *Dansk musiktidsskrift*, Vol. 45, No. 7, 1969, pp. 146–49.

sketches, a short score, and a full score; and he often revises works, usually only slightly, after hearing them performed. In the last two decades he has completed over eighty works, from short *a cappella* songs to large-scale symphonies. For some time he has had enough commissions tentatively accepted to keep him busy for years, although he has also written works which nobody commissioned but which he simply wanted to write.

Most important among the compositions from the last two decades are a dozen string quartets; several other chamber works; three solo organ works; *Tempo variable*, the last work to be subtitled 'Symphonic Metamorphosis'; *Diafora*, for strings; several concertos; Chamber Symphonies Nos. 2 and 3; Symphonies Nos. 9, 10 and 11 (for full orchestra); and five Preludes (for small orchestra). His Tenth Symphony was written for the Detroit Symphony Orchestra and was first performed by Sixten Ehrling and that orchestra when he was its principal conductor, and is Holmboe's only work to have been commissioned by an American institution.

Over the past fifteen years, it has been my pleasure and honour to study and write about the music of Vagn Holmboe and to get to know him personally. To describe his character would be as difficult as to describe his music, neither of which I wish to do here to any further extent. Nonetheless, two passages in the article already cited, written by Thorkild Bjørnvig for *Dansk musiktidsskrift* on the occasion of Holmboe's sixtieth birthday, are worth quoting as the conclusion to this biographical sketch of the composer. The first refers to 1958, when Holmboe had agreed to set to music Bjørnvig's cantata text for an anniversary of Aarhus University.

> The first get-togethers and trips to the University, where Holmboe made himself familiar with the acoustical environment to the Ciceronian accompaniment of his text-writer, took place in nothing but deep seriousness – until on the fourth trip I unfortunately set off some half-disguised jokes and cracks, which nevertheless fell like sparks in a room loaded with petrol fumes and unleashed explosions in the form of jokes that the sheepish text-writer had never dreamed could pass through the lips on this serious and imposing visage.
>
> In Vagn Holmboe I found the ruthless intellectual integrity, the first-hand relationship to phenomena, the unfailing aim for

the heart of problems from no matter what angle, which characterise significant artists as well as philosophers and scientists, and
which are features they have in common. Often it became hard
for me to follow his thought process, mostly on account of its
formidable speed, the lightning-quick tempo with which it
reached its target. However, I usually understood the result, even
though I was glad when the lightning – for the sake of the company – turned back to the starting-point and instead of a dynamic zig-zag, turned itself, with an abundance of pedagogical
patience, into a maze or a spiral. Then I learned a lot.

ACKNOWLEDGEMENTS

I wish to thank the publisher Gyldendal for permission to print the translation of *Music – the Inexplicable*; Edition Wilhelm Hansen for permission to print the translation of 'Epilogue' and 'On the Experiencing of Time', which are taken from Vagn Holmboe's book *Mellemspil*, which they published in 1961; the Danish Cultural Institute (Det danske selskab) for permission to reprint 'In Memory of Carl Nielsen', translated by Erik Ruusunen, published by them in 1964. 'Human Responsibility and Artistic Freedom' first appeared in Torben Meyer, Josef Müller-Marein and Hannes Reinhardt (eds.), *Musikalske selvportrætter*, Jul. Gjellerups forlag, Copenhagen, 1966, and 'A Little String Trio' was published in Ib Sinding Jensen (ed.), *Min debut*, distributed by *Jyllands-Posten* for 1 January 1966.

I wish also to thank Vagn Holmboe, Martin Anderson, Brian Duke and Guy Rickards for their valuable assistance, the McMaster University Arts Research Board for its support, and Robert Simpson for contributing the Foreword to this book. Help with the proof-reading was provided by Guy Rickards and David Brown.

PAUL RAPOPORT
Hamilton, Ontario
30 July 1987

MUSIC -
THE INEXPLICABLE

Previous page:
Holmboe, photographed at dusk on the Faroe Islands in 1982 (Meta May Holmboe)

PRELUDE

'Culture depends not on what it gives but on what it demands of humanity.'   ANTOINE DE SAINT-EXUPÉRY (1900-1944)

'Beautiful are those things we see, more beautiful are those we understand; but by far the most beautiful are those which we do not comprehend.'   NIELS STEENSEN (1638-1686)

Music as Part of our Culture

These two quotations strike me as important, for they touch on problems which concern us all, which despite their apparently opposing views together suggest those conditions which determine our cultural setting.

Exupéry's words are plain: without demands, without challenges to the individual, a culture cannot endure. It may well live on awhile by drawing nourishment from what has been handed down, but in doing that it becomes purely passive. Its powers of renewal and development are broken, and it will finally disintegrate or be overthrown.

Steensen's statement may possibly be taken in various ways, but I can understand the remark only as an acknowledgement that there will always be incomprehensible things behind the comprehensible, no matter how far we progress in our understanding, and that the 'most beautiful things' will always be outside the control of thought and word.

For me there is no doubt that a human being is a creative being, that human development depends to a large extent on an interrelation of thought and play, indeed, that our entire existence is constrained by the need to construct a cosmos from chaos, whether this cosmos has an artistic character or not.

The creative will expresses itself as a demand for personal effort, a challenge to our ability and energy. A touch of play may enter into the work we are occupied with; it becomes easier and at the same time gains a particular significance for us, because it gives us an inner satisfaction when we think it is well done.

And so it matters little whether we are plastering a house, sweeping a path, washing up dishes or singing or whistling some spontaneous melody – only that we are involved in what we are undertaking with our whole mind.

Music is part of our culture, and it demands some effort from those who will not be content with superficial enjoyment and passive stagnation. To be sure, music is a readily accessible art form for all who have open ears: people have in their own voices an instrument which at will they can use tolerably well, and which in any case can give the performer considerable satisfaction and delight quite directly. There are very many opportunities to hear music free in our culture, and in urban society they are almost unavoidable: it is there on streets and squares, in supermarkets, from radio speakers and from transistors.

On closer study, music is just as complex in our culture as it can be immediate and direct in its effect on the listener. The person who wants to *know* something about music and is willing to make a personal effort to gain this knowledge must be prepared for a series of demands which will vary with the subject and goal, but which leads to consequences of rather large scope.

My purpose here is to shed light on the relationship of people to music and the possibility of their accepting and thus expressing their nature through musical experience, whether this experience is achieved by creative work, by active collaboration, or by participation as a listener. I will make an attempt at giving an account of some of the relationships which make music meaningful in this way.

This is directly impossible, since the abstract content of music does not have a meaning which can be expressed with words or which can be justified or proved. On the other hand, the particular piece of music which I am listening to (or have a vivid memory of) can be meaningful for me, even though this too cannot be explained very precisely at all. Much has been written about music in the course of time; the subject has been thoroughly treated in all its many aspects – theoretical, mathematical, formal and historical – just as many flowery words have been written and spoken on the aesthetics and emotional content of music. But we cannot come to know much about music's true nature; and we experience the truth of Mendelssohn's aphorism that much has been uttered and little said about music.

The Musical Phenomenon

If I would like here to approach the land of musical experience and what conditions it, a land that undoubtedly has roots deep in the human psyche and where I have only a layman's insight, it is clear to me that I will often find myself in an extremely narrow passage between Scylla and Charybdis, between the cool assessment of a professional and the bottomless pit of the amateur.

But I must persevere. First I shall claim that music is something other and more than the sum of its components, that even the most thorough, meticulous analysis leaves something inexplicable. Analysis of this inexplicable aspect is precluded, since it comes to musical life only in its own time-span and therefore manifests itself and is capable of having a direct effect on people only when the music is being played.

This phenomenon, so common in all art, is especially perceptible with music. What goes by when we listen can certainly be taken in with lightning speed; as a rule it happens fairly consciously. But if we attempt to analyse what has been taken in *while the music is being heard*, we can of course manage to gain some kind of knowledge about these matters, but we can at most experience fragments of the whole, for we lose the continuity and thus also the possibility of experiencing the musical substance, the meaningful part – which can be grasped in full only in the time-span of the music itself. We are forced either to stop the course of the music (even if for quite a short time) so as to be able to analyse it – and will thereby kill off the possibility of a direct experience – or we must give up analysing while the music is being heard, to be able to experience it in its own dimension, in its particular progress through time.

We may thus speak of a paradoxical, or rather a complementary relationship: experiencing music and analysing it are mutually exclusive. This does not mean 'either/or', e.g., that analysis in itself hinders musical experience, nor that the efforts of the intellect must stop when music is heard. Active mental functioning is an important precondition for the listener to be able to gain a full understanding of a piece of music while it is being heard. Subsequently, a complicated intellectual process, a detailed analysis of the piece of music, can itself elucidate any relevant compositional, stylistic or formal problems when this analysis, it should be noted, does not coincide with the performance. The prerequisite for a musical experience is thus that some form of analytical process be done with when the music is heard, so that, instead of hindering, it will clear away obstacles and promote that insight which determines the experience of an artistic reality.

That music is something other and more than the sum of its parts is obviously an assumption; but I consider it to be self-evident, just as evident as the fact that the concept of a human being is something above and beyond the sum of bone structure, blood circulation, nervous system, organs, etc. – namely, *life*.

Just like the human being, music is built out of analysable elements: a rhythmic figure, a motive, a chord; but by themselves, these details have no actual existence as music. In themselves they are lifeless building blocks; what we call music can arise only in connection with other elements, which means that there has occurred a wonderful transformation of these individual parts which are now assembled into a whole and gain quality and substance, gain life.

But all these concepts are suspended in mid-air. For in a purely musical context, expressions like *quality, substance, insight* and *experience* simply cannot be defined or even made verbally comprehensible with any sort of precision.

Admittedly, it is possible to get inside the magic circle where these concepts have an existence and where they are self-evident; but we stand helpless if faced, for example, with having to explain which qualities have substance, or describe with words the insight which a musical experience can give, whether it is universal or exclusively personal.

To grasp the nettle I shall mentally go right back to the beginning, to the music before it was written down and to the composer before he wrote it down. This I can do only on the basis of personal experience and memories of the various creative processes I have been through, but with the thought that the subjective will perhaps be the most instructive way to the general, and that with this background I can, if not define, then at least approach the problems of these concepts, and cast a little light on them.

First Movement
THE COMPOSER

Unconscious and Conscious States

I am quite certain that no one, not even the individual composer, can obtain so sure and clear a glimpse into the genesis of a musical work that a precise explanation can be given of the way things arise and progress, or of the forces that are the cause of the way things go on the often long road from the first ideas to the finished work of art.

Some things, of course, may be remembered, especially from the periods in the process which are dominated by conscious deliberation, by feelings and actions. But even under those circumstances all one's attention has been centred on abstract musical matters, concentrated on turning some notes into an artistic whole. That is why only single, often irrelevant observations will be remembered – incidental events whose significance and relevance are all too easily rationalised.

Furthermore, in genuinely creative moments self-awareness is temporarily out of action. Even if you try to think back a very short time after having composed, a dense fog will lie over the process and thus over what really occurred.

When you work intensely on a piece of music, there is a strong need for an attention of the will, a conscious concentration on the matter itself with all its complexity. But beyond that – and this is what is important – you are in a self-forgetting state where any objectives and desires, hopes and ambitions disappear. You are no longer conscious of yourself and feel like a passive tool, filled with sounds which contain on their own, as it were, a forming power. This feeling, that it is the music itself which determines its course, is basically an illusion; I will have more to say about it in what follows.

The two states, the actively concentrating and the passively receptive, may obviously alternate with much rapidity, which can be noticed only later on, because one is not conscious of

37

physical time when engrossed in work. It is thus impossible to have so certain a knowledge of creative forces that it can be formulated in words.

Fragments without the whole and its continuity may emerge in our consciousness when we try to think back. But, as with an iceberg, most of it remains hidden, and we can only infer the nature of what is hidden and speculate about its extent. We must realise that observations on the events, thoughts and conceptions we can have about these conditions can be recalled in the memory only up to a certain point. Considering their true nature, they are a result of personal experiences and therefore must remain either fragments for reflection or reconstructed reports, when we try to objectivise and describe them.

On the other hand, I have no doubt that experiences of this kind are possible for everyone, regardless of the concrete connection with apparent aims. It is immaterial whether art is involved or not. Thus we will also be able to call subjective (although never merely private) the experiences which, like those mentioned, are involved in what lies behind musical creation, and the attempts to account for them.

Considering that my subject is after all a universal human concern, there are special reasons for a closer inquiry and, too, for renewed attempts to isolate this hidden and inviolable territory from the artistic side. As I have said, it cannot be described or analysed directly, but I can throw some light on the matter via the individual developments and sporadic fragments which are preserved in my memory and of which I will now give some examples – still realising that the events which strike me as important and which have possibly led to the greatest artistic results are far more difficult to explain than those many more activities which are routine but which therefore should also be mentioned.

It has happened that as a composer I have been through experiences which are completely outside time and place. Perhaps some vague thing or other has been stirring for a while in the background of my consciousness or in the wholly unconscious; but whatever may be going on, something can arise with surprising suddenness, altering my normal working rhythm and forcing me into a new situation.

You become conscious of the surprise only later, for while you are in the midst of it, your surroundings disappear in front of you – and then where you are is quite a minor matter, whether you are walking, standing in a tram or sitting in your room. Under all these circumstances your consciousness is momentarily out of action, or acts in close contact with the unconscious.

I do not know whether it is a short flash or whether it lasts some while, and I am not really interested. Moreover, without warning I feel I am in a large space which has nothing to do with where I actually am. This space is infinite and I myself am a part of it. The space is perceived as somewhat soft and luminous, but is without dimensions, without colour, form, or shape of any kind.

That is all I can recount.

Afterwards the space closes around you, or you become conscious of yourself with an indescribable but pleasant lightness of mind. You know with certainty that *something* has been born, something that has no sound, thought nor form; and your passive receptivity is transformed, as consciousness awakens, into some outward-directed activity. You *must* then realise something or other in some medium or other, which here means in music.

From this situation to the completely finished work the paths are manifold and contorted. In a particular case I remember it turning into an orchestral work, a symphony, without my knowing one note of the music. It stood quite clear as a larger totality in my consciousness; I knew how it had to be, but not how I could best realise this knowledge and get the work down intact on paper. But sounds streamed forth now as if on their own; they sang in me, and I had to use all the ability and technique I had, and soon, to organise and sift this stream, knowing well from experience that at the moment when contact with the original experience is weakening, it is very easy for me to be led astray, away from the totality of which the experience gave me an inkling and which has now become the goal for all my endeavours.[1]

It takes months to get a grasp of things, to follow the course of which I have such a sure, although only half-conscious, knowledge. It is like following a thread of Ariadne, always losing

[1] The experience discussed here involved Symphony No. 6, Op. 43 (1947).

it, and yet strenuously finding the way back to it, in order to be led forward once more.

In the long process of working which follows such an experience, the unconscious and the clearly conscious are not separated from each other. Each kind of impulse gives rise to the other, or else arises spontaneously and miraculously with no apparent connection with the context. The connection turns up only later when one goes over the matter critically.

The conscious work is a stripping-away of irrelevant ideas, a revising of details, maybe a listening for what instrumental sound is being heard by the inner ear. Intellect and reason judge proportions and many practical details: balance of form and sound, the range of the instruments and their technical possibilities. There may occur a certain conflict between the feeling for the character of the material – its qualities and tensions – on the one hand, and reasoned decisions about the extent of the form on the other, and only a superior feeling for both 'points of view' may lead to a successful result.

From time to time, impassable obstructions stop things by blocking further work. You suspect the way in which the stubborn knot can be loosened and how a particular passage can be shaped, but it seems impossible to get the sounds to mould themselves: thus the necessity of continuing on the other side of the blockade in order to avoid undue delays. Afterwards it turns out that in the meantime the knot has untied itself, and that now the missing passage can be filled in and written down with the greatest ease.

Analysis of the flickering shifts between the unconscious and the conscious while the work is going on is precluded, because the whole self is occupied, even engulfed, in the work and it is thus outside the control of the intellect. And if afterwards we try to analyse the situation, that too is precluded, for then the door is slammed shut against the unconscious part of the team. Only a small part of the events, i.e., the purely intellectual parts, can be remembered and analysed *post factum.*

One knows, of course, that one has been writing away, often exasperatedly trying to preserve the totality while struggling with especially important details. Only when that eruptive, half-conscious stage is over does the working process become one of finalising the material in the context of instrumental or vocal sound. And this process is influenced by all these considerations and reflections, for now that the totality is given and formulated, it is possible to go on and listen clearly and consciously to all the details and their effect in sound.

Work and Crises

Unfortunately there are periods in life when things will not go right, when everything that you try goes wrong; and so the difficulties quickly pile up and make any work impossible. You can try to forget and flee from the music, but you are pursued everywhere by the same unbearable problems which beset you and which you can neither loosen nor be loosened from. Such a situation can be rather depressing; gradually you become afraid that you will stagnate completely, afraid that it is all over forever if these problems are not solved. There is silence in your head where music should be sounding, there is emptiness where there should be fullness, and desperation where there should be serenity.

Fortunately, it often all lasts only a short period, either right after the completion of a large work which has exhausted your strength, or for a few unfortunate days when you can't quite get anything done and when your otherwise much-needed self-criticism turns into a destructive beast. In any case it is futile to sit with your arms folded and give up everything or hope that something will happen. You have to grab hold of something, almost anything at all. Over the course of time I have tried many things before eventually succeeding in finding two possibilities for overcoming these difficulties.

Often I have tried to work my way through the crisis, to write and throw out and keep going even though it seems hopeless and the situation can expand beyond all proportions into a real Jacob's struggle.[2] And you discover that it is not in the actual musical difficulties that the problems lie, but in yourself. It takes not only strength and will, but also much patience for the lost contact to be found. And unfortunately things do not always work out that way.

But in recent years another possibility has become more useful: I ignore as much as possible the situation and my own sluggishness and occupy myself with some kind of unimportant business. For example, I can revise an earlier work, set up a score for a projected piece of music which nonetheless must be written

[2] [See Genesis, 32:24 *et seq.*]

sooner or later, or perhaps merely go for walks, read books, write letters. The problems are not disposed of or forgotten; I have merely tried to push them out of my thoughts for a while.

Now it happens that, like most other composers, consciously or unconsciously I always have music in me, regardless of what I am otherwise working at – little detached notes and rhythms to which I normally do not pay much attention, especially when I am intensely occupied mentally or physically. But over the years I have found that work which is unimportant and not very strenuous the effect of a key in a locked door, the door that leads in to the contacts that are otherwise unavailable. Then it may happen that all the problems melt away as if they had never existed, and that some of the lifeless or merely unheeded notes and rhythms that have been going through my head begin to take on life, so that they become loaded with a power that brings them forward to full consciousness and makes them 'sing' in me.

These previously trivial notes with their various intervals and rhythms suddenly become alive, charged with energy and with a compelling demand to release and develop their unknown forces; such psychological phenomena quite pass my understanding. And it is not really my business to look for a possible explanation for them. My need and duty are to identify with the given possibilities, to bring my intellect to accept with due humility what is felt to be a gift of grace, and then to become immersed in my work and to stick to it, whatever it may cost.

If the situation has previously been insoluble, it can now be solved at once; and if I do not have any problem at the time, these notes that have come alive will suggest entirely new possibilities for musical development, because they are now suddenly grasped as parts of a larger, perhaps still unknown whole.

As an example I can mention a situation from 1950.

The Lives of Motives

I was standing at the back of a tramcar, and without apparent cause, a little motive-complex emerged in my consciousness. There did not seem to be anything particularly interesting about it, other than that it continued to push itself forward. It had nothing to do with the rhythm of the tramcar nor with the people around me; it was not inspired by the boring professional meeting from which I was on my way home. But the motivic idea would not leave me in peace. It grew and developed to such an extent that I had to begin as quickly as possible to write something down so that it would not disappear or grow wild in my consciousness. (I can never get away from an inveterate fear that such musical impulses will escape yet again.)

But I wrote down as much as could go on the back of a matchbox I had in my pocket. When I got home, I went into what I had written, and soon I became certain that one of the many little round note-combinations, which ordinarily would often be ignored, had been given an astounding power that made possible a long course of development.

In this case it turned into more than half a year's hard work, which again resulted in a symphony.[3]

And another case, a little earlier, but perfectly parallel: I was on my way to a gathering of some friends when a melodic line emerged in my consciousness. I listened, rummaged in my pockets and found pencil and paper to write down the essential bit, a motive with a striking undulating rhythm. And again I had a kernel which possessed the magical power to fill my mind with living gestures, with a strong urge to follow up the motive, to release its latent powers and create a large-scale work out of this seed. And all this had happened without an apparent emotional cause or any other recollected influence.[4]

Here is a third case, which occurred a few years ago.

I was about to finish off a string quartet but, just as so often in the past, a motive, or rather a sound emerged in my consciousness, something very light and transparent but nonetheless penetrating. It had nothing to do with the work which I had before me, so I merely jotted down a few notes on a scrap of music paper to get it out of my head and get on with the work on my quartet.

The quartet was completed and I still had the desire to write something; but it had to be something quite different, a choral or orchestral work, anything at all – simply not another string quartet. I played a little with the musical thought that came up

---

[3] Symphony No. 7, Op. 50 (1950). [An analysis of the Seventh Symphony may be found in Paul Rapoport, *Opus Est*, Kahn & Averill, London, 1978.]

[4] The 'undulating' motive first comes forward some way into the First String Quartet, Op. 46 (1948–49).

so inconveniently and which insisted on seeing the light of day; and the worst part of it was that it sounded like a quartet. I tried to think orchestrally, to make the motive develop with the rich sonorous possibilities of large orchestral forces; but it would not work. A month went by with frustrating ideas and hopeless attempts to use this motive, which now pushed itself more and more forward and was already expanding and budding with new motives, but without having its own body to secure the existence and life of this indomitable will.

Finally I gave up and decided, since it could not be anything else, to start on a new quartet. And after that everything fell into place, my mind was relieved, and the work went like a charm. For what now had to be written down was luminously clear to me: not just the original idea, which in this case is the beginning of the quartet, but also the essential ideas of the several following movements with all their contrasts and possibilities of development.[5]

Musical Ideas and their Origins

When I am working on a piece of music I am usually so busy, even engrossed in my work, that most considerations and events float by me without my paying attention to them. They register, perhaps, but are plainly forgotten at once or are pushed aside and relegated to an obscure place in the background of one's consciousness. But now, when I try to think back, I believe I have experienced huge differences in intensity and quality in what are called musical ideas and their possible background.

Some ideas seem to come from the unknown layers in the mind where thought does not penetrate, and one may only guess that a force must grow and mature awhile before it can break through to the conscious mind, where it is formulated as a musical idea. On the other hand, other ideas hardly seem to have their point of departure very far at all under the mind's surface and can often – apparently, anyway – be traced back to concrete antecedents: a particular frame of mind or an external influence. However this works, these layers in the mind, half conscious and half brought into consciousness, are dominated by intellect and

---

[5] The two String Quartets discussed here are Nos. 13 and 14, Opp. 124 and 125 (both of 1975). [This is not the only occasion on which Holmboe has been forced from within, so to speak, to write a string quartet.]

emotion in constant interplay. Emotions such as like/dislike, happiness/sadness, satisfaction/wonder are mixed with thoughts such as yes/no, must/must not, good/bad in unbroken interaction amid seriousness, leisure and work. And this dialogue goes on constantly during work on a piece of music, whether or not there is any demonstrable impact from outside.

Lastly, I also know which kind of artistic activity is from start to finish a predominantly intellectual matter, almost exclusively based on musical and technical skill. Later I shall go further into this state of affairs, which very often results in what have been called 'pot-boilers'.

First I must mention the obvious: that sound, the audible, may be the catalyst for a composer. It can happen in many ways. Nature has its own sounds which can produce impulses, or music from a radio or a recording can come into the room where you are sitting.

Then it happens that you listen with only half an ear, for you have discovered that in the midst of everything you yourself are forming some music in ways that have nothing remotely to do with the sounds or the music which is going by your ears and which, as quickly as possible, you now ignore in order to follow your own musical train of thought. You can even go around humming something quite different from what is filling your mind, and thereby let the external music, which is so unimportant to you, be a mental cover for the music that is still not clearly formulated in your consciousness.

I am well aware that over the last couple of centuries the piano has been the most important medium in getting the composer's mind going. The composer might play others' works to get on the right track, or combine a few random notes in the hope that they will start something and develop into meaningful music.

The piano is, indeed, the composer's usual working instrument although seldom an absolute necessity, since the real musical working process goes on inside, independently of external sound. In addition, the sound of the piano can be extremely disturbing when you are not working on piano music at the time but, let us say, are looking for a certain combination of instruments, a particular orchestral sound, or are shaping a passage which you hear as vocal or choral.

I myself use the piano rather often but do not basically 'hear' it as an instrument. After having played through a composition to gain some sense of its physical sound, I have sometimes discovered that the piano was terribly out of tune. But this could not disturb me, because in my inner ear I heard only the sound of the instruments for which I was writing and completely ignored the piano's mistuned pitches. Under other circumstances the very slightest drift in pitch would have an inordinately irritating effect.

For me the piano acts chiefly as a court of control for what I am working on and thereafter test at the instrument as well as I can there. True enough, it can sometimes inspire me or set me going if I let my fingers play with the keys with no real purpose other than the quiet hope that something will crop up. It does happen that the first sparks jump out here, although rarely without some vague prior notion at least of some indefinite music lying far back in one's consciousness. But it also happens that nothing comes about.

I remember, for instance, a situation where I had just finished a large-scale composition. I was fatigued and still filled with physical inertia; I did everything to forget the finished work, to get it right out of my consciousness to make room for something new. It is, by the way, a well–known situation: after completing a work, you look involuntarily and immediately for something new, just a little germ of something new, a sign that things are still alive inside, to avoid the feeling of emptiness that so often follows long mental exertion.

Now it could begin – but could it, in fact? I sat down at the piano and had a go, but nothing came of my fingers' fumbling sound-play, no matter how many attempts I made to awaken the slumbering powers, to bring some new music to life. I tried and tried, more and more desperately, and listened for what might be a little spark of life somewhere or other. But no! Finally I had to give up. And it was not pleasant, to put it mildly, for spiritually I found myself in an endless desert, forsaken by everything and everyone, alone with my shortcomings, filled with fear of the impending sterility, the empty space.

Under no circumstances could I remain there, and I was quite sure that I had to pull myself together, get my will involved in order to overcome this desperate state. But how?

A few days went by, taken up with ordinary tasks, and I was certainly not pleasant company during this period. So I sat down with a crossword puzzle. But it wasn't solved at one sitting, for just as I was looking for a synonym I had to jump up: one of the little motives to which I had earlier tried to give artificial respiration but which had slipped through my fingers, had begun to 'sing' in my mind. And that is tantamount to saying that it had been transformed, had gained life, and in some miraculous manner had become part of a larger whole.

This wholeness was probably still unconscious; I *knew* that it was there but not what it was like. Actually I did know, but not where the little life-giving and life-given germ belonged in the unknown sequence of events. All this I discovered only eventually, as I continued to work. I recognised things, so to speak, now that the music had begun to flow and the latent power had been freed.[6]

This case is far from being unique. And if you have gone this far, the work can go like a charm, at least in the beginning. How things will grow becomes clearer and clearer. You notice the music shaping itself and do not know whether the music or you yourself is shaping its growth. But there must always be fresh suggestions of internal 'singing' if the task is not to proceed sluggishly, come to a standstill, or, to put it bluntly, become routine and worthless. As happens in the fortunate cases, a chain reaction of ideas or impulses must occur, everything having sprung forth from the original material or potentially related to (but rich in contrast with) it, while at the same time you are working intensely with all kinds of technical problems.

Sometimes there is real excitement about what is to come next, about how it can go further. Deep inside, your suspicions may be right, but you are not completely sure and are often surprised at the solution to the problems, at the result which later proves to be quite obvious.

When it comes to the necessary cessation of work from day to day, I have found that it is best to leave it at an incomplete point. An unsolved problem then becomes an irritant like a grain of sand in an oyster – so that you must ceaselessly let your thoughts circle around the unfinished business and keep all the possibilities open. If, on the other hand, it is a matter of a longer

---

[6] [These events involved the completion of Symphony No. 8, Op. 56 (1951–52) and the starting of *Moya*, Op. 57, a set of songs for mezzo-soprano and piano (1952). Something similar occurred with the completion of String Quartet No. 3, Op. 48 (1949) and the starting of *Suono da Bardo*, Op. 49, for piano (1949–50).]

span of time – a trip or something comparable – the excitement cannot be maintained, and it becomes a burning question how you can once more find a way into the characteristic spirit of the work and get back the lost overview.

Such are the consequences of carrying music around inside you nearly constantly, whatever the undertaking at hand. The music also lives on in the mind outside the actual working process. Awkward interruptions and lengthy, time-consuming or demanding duties may therefore sometimes give rise to conflicts, as much internal as involving those around you. In contrast, routine, everyday requirements do not cause trouble, even though they may be carried out with a certain absent-mindedness.

Thus it is my experience that you may easily peel away the habit-layers of the mind and immediately get inside the spirit of the work when you sit down again to continue working. But if you have been genuinely interrupted, it may take both time and energy to get into the work once more.

It is not my intention, incidentally, to go over the innumerable external and internal difficulties that are unavoidable when it comes to working on an artistic level. If they cannot be resolved, it is almost always because some ability is lacking – knowledge or insight – and thus it would merely be a question of rattling off the identical technical, musical or psychological details.

But I have come up against one special difficulty which – far from being due to a lack of ideas – stems from too many concurrent ideas and which therefore must be mentioned.

In the midst of working on a large-scale piece I have had misgivings because I suddenly have two possibilities, two equally good ideas to choose between – and it is an uncomfortable dilemma. I am required to choose, to listen for the only correct solution, and I make my choice to the best of my ability. But it does not work out. The material seems weighty enough but cannot be fitted into the whole. It is continuously pushed out, proves unsuitable and, finally, when every hope seems dashed, must be rejected.

There is then an obligation to take up the other possibility for consideration. But, unfortunately, precisely the same thing happens now: it does not belong there. Despite all mistakes, your thoughts circle constantly around these ideas and their possibilities. Both should actually be suitable, both are related to the rest of the music, but neither of them can be used in the given whole.

You look for other material but find only a sickening emptiness. You become embittered but cannot get away from the original ideas.

I have been up against this dilemma several times, and each time a little miracle has occurred: at some point or other the two different possibilities became fused into one in my consciousness.

How it came about I do not know, but they became mixed and firmly united. They turned into one independent and completely new motive-complex. After that there was no obstruction, no problem of adjustment. The answer was as obvious as if there had never been a question.[7]

Working to Commission

There is, to be sure, a general assumption that commissioned works must be markedly routine pot-boilers for a composer, but that is far from always being the case. A commission can in itself provide stimulation, whether it comes from performers who want something new for their repertory or from a more official quarter: a music society, an orchestra, a festival, or the Radio's music division.[8] Such stimulation can be fed by, among other things, the recollection of the special tone of skilful performers and their way of playing, which can directly create music in the inner ear, or by an exciting instrumental combination which is felt as a challenge to the degree of one's command of the material.

Incidentally, of the approximately thirty works I have written in the past six or seven years, 26 of them have seen the light of day as a result of more or less official commissions.[9] Institutions, ensembles and individual performers from various countries have commissioned or requested music of widely differing kinds, from symphonies and choral works to solo concertos and chamber music. From such a relatively large basis of experience alone, a discussion of the problems that may arise in this connection seems both relevant and necessary.

[7] The difficulties discussed here arose with the third movement of Symphony No. 8, Op. 56 (1951–52).

[8] [Here Holmboe refers to Danish Radio, which, like other European broadcasting organisations, is a source of much musical activity, including commissions.]

[9] [That is, up to 1981, when the original Danish version of this book was completed.]

When a commission is accepted, most often there are the same possibilities as usual, but with certain modifications. If it is performer-colleagues who are asking for a piece of music which they can and will play, you can sometimes wait until something has ripened inside you. In this respect the situation is not too different from a composition that is completely open, for you are committed to, or inspired by, only the soloist who is to play the music or the ensemble which is formed by these colleagues. Some years ago two prominent musicians asked me to write a piece for trumpet and organ – an unfamiliar instrumental combination for me, and one which created a quite special situation, not least because two such different instruments inevitably had to affect, or even determine, the course of the music.

But I took up this challenge, threw myself into work, and soon had the impression that I myself had chosen the two instruments in order to conquer unknown territory. Problems arose, but of a purely musical nature, and I forgot about it being a commission until the piece was at last finished.[10]

But a request may also come from one of the established ensembles with which one is quite familiar and with whose sound and manner of playing one has identified for a long time – a string quartet, for example. Such a request may act like an inoculation. You do not know whether it will 'take', but you are completely free with respect to the task; you can give yourself up to the music and renew yourself in the attempt to master this, the most difficult of all musical media.[11]

But there may also be requests to write an orchestral or choral work, often of a given duration and to a given deadline. If such a commission is accepted, problems may arise, especially if there is not enough time for the material to reach the necessary maturation in your mind. Then you may get in a jam and have to fall back on your skill and your technique, and hope that impulses and ideas will turn up when you get down to work, which fortunately can happen.

But if not, you must grapple with things as best you can, and

---

[10] [*Triade*, Op. 123 (1974–75); the work subsequently underwent some revision, although not because it was a commission.]

[11] [Holmboe's long association with the Copenhagen String Quartet has undoubtedly been a stimulus for some of his finest music.]

in the worst instances it goes wrong: the notes refuse to turn into music, there is no depth or resonance behind them, and the work becomes insipid and dreary, ending up as noticeably routine and commonplace.

That situation you avoid as much as possible. You feel it as a serious artistic defeat from which you cannot extricate yourself, regardless of whether you have finished a sizable task in a short time, whether your working morale is still good, and whether on the surface the piece is fairly smooth and attractive. You see that you have forsaken an indispensable prerequisite for all creative art of any significance, which is that your entire person, physical as well as mental, conscious as well as unconscious, should be and must be part of the work. You know deep within that this has not been the case, and you wish only to toss the whole thing out, to forget all about it. You wish that you had not accepted the commission, even if it may have been hard to say 'No'.

By this I do not mean that the capacity to think is without importance when you are writing music – only that it cannot work satisfactorily without the participation of other attributes. Musical thinking is, on the contrary, most important and in the end has a crucial influence on whether the music is completed in a way that takes care of the original ideas. These ideas, which are often born quite unconsciously, cannot be realised in a score without the capacity to think musically.

Musical Thinking

Just as we may think in words and connect them to form meaningful sentences, we may also think in sounds and combine them to form meaningful wholes. That a composer can hear sounds in the inner ear is both natural and necessary, and is probably no more unusual than that a poet who thinks a poem can hear the words in the inner ear.

Inner hearing is essential, but it turns into musical thinking only when you are activated mentally and are not merely listening to the sound of the words or the notes. You can mentally combine notes into constructive unities, connect them with varied rhythms and sonorities, have combinations of notes arise, resolve them, and form new ones — you can develop them, shape and finalise their form in a purely mental process.

Thus we can speak of musical thinking, and this process is

plainly parallel with the poet's or scientist's thinking in words, images, formulae or abstract concepts.

Yet there is one substantial difference between verbal and musical thinking, although it may be due to a dispute over terms: whereas words may be combined in a logical sequence to form sentences, we can scarcely speak in the same way of logic in music. Music is an abstract medium which cannot deny, confirm or prove; but it can be meaningful in its combinations, be significant, have coherence, and be so convincingly consistent that a musical process might very easily be confused with verbal logic.

Dreams

It does happen that I dream music, which must properly be thought of as diametrically opposed to clear, conscious musical thinking. Nonetheless, I do not feel they are opposed in the morning when I have a precise and detailed impression of an entire composition (never heard before) which I feel was thoroughly worked out in the dream. Probably what usually happens is that only some few notes are remembered and perhaps are noted down and then forgotten because they do not seem to have any coherence, or perhaps because in the light of day they prove to be diffuse commonplaces. But two or three times it has happened that I have written down large portions of a dream composition from memory. One of my symphonies was like that, with all the essential parts of its themes, motives, its form and instrumentation written down and worked out further in accordance with what was dreamed. Even the notation was so clear that it often seemed that I was writing a copy.

I have not been too worried about a potential connection between dreams and the unconscious, because first and foremost it was the results which interested me and with which, regardless of their causes, I had to work further. As I have said, the largest part of the dream music consisted of fragments whose meaning and connections I did not grasp and which I still wrote down but forgot about right away again because they did not seem to be of any use.[12]

But some years ago it happened that I became uneasy in the midst of working on a large-scale orchestral work, a symphony.

[12] The 'dreamed music' became the Fifth Symphony, Op. 35 (1944).

I thought I knew the main theme a little too well and was not sure whether it was an unconscious quotation from another composer. Where did I know it from? I could not remember having heard it before, and yet it was extremely familiar, now that I came to think about it. So I went and leafed through my old notes to have a closer look at the scraps of music which had occurred to me or which I had dreamed over the course of time.

And there the theme turned up, if in a somewhat incomplete notation – something I had dreamed years earlier, written down, and since then forgotten completely. I searched further and found more undeveloped sketches, written down months or even years apart. There was no connection between these sketches in my memory, and in any case I had not been able to co-ordinate them before they were forgotten again. But now, from an entirely new point and in light of the large-scale context with which I was working, I could see that it was a matter of different sides and degrees of development of one and the same motive-complex, and I understood why the music could flow forward so freely, as if by itself.[13]

I can interpret the events only thus: that the material matures slowly, outside clear and active consciousness, and from embryonic states turns up intermittently in an increasingly more developed guise, but with no audible connection to anything familiar, and thus always pushed out of the mind as unusable. Eventually it comes right up to the surface of consciousness, thanks to an inspiring experience which has the effect of a triggering catalyst. The material becomes charged with energy and achieves 'idea' status and coherence, now that it is perceived within a larger whole.

Perhaps the kind of dream that can later take on a certain quality in consciousness is the exception. On the other hand, it is an experience which I know many have had: in sleep unconscious energies may be freed from all the everyday trifles and solve current problems directly, make simple and comprehensible matters which before were impossibly complicated. It is my firm belief that without sleep's accumulation of energy, my music would lack an important dimension. In sleep I experience not only physical and mental rest but also an unconscious activity

---

[13] The allusion here is again to the Sixth Symphony, Op. 43 [*cf.* p. 39].

on which I depend and to which I attribute the utmost significance for creative work.

Nature

Composers sometimes come up against the question of whether nature is an inspiration. Without really knowing what is actually meant by 'nature' I must answer 'No'.

Like so many other people, I am strongly attached to the natural world which surrounds us, of which we human beings are a part, and which I wish to be saved from ugly and destructive interference. And so I also have an eye for the external in nature, the picturesque, for grandiose or gentle views of landscapes, for distinctive details, mountain masses and salt marshes, forests and heaths. But all this has much less significance for me than that which is inherent in nature: the unique existence and life rhythm of plants, their blooming and wilting; the lives of animals and birds; the change of weather and of the seasons; the endlessness, complexity, power and peacefulness of the sea. This feeling for and living in nature and its rhythms has given me the sensation of being not just an outside observer but in the most proper sense part of that very nature which surrounds me.

For me, to go out in nature is to take a spiritual bath, both a physical and a mental renewal and strengthening, regardless of whether I am active – planting trees, felling them, and chopping firewood – or whether I am merely an observer of the myriad small wonders in which nature is so rich. But I am not aware of any direct musical inspiration from nature, unless using birdsong in a composition is to be called inspiration.

Undoubtedly this is an entirely personal statement. Other people may have a quite different relationship to nature, which for them may be directly inspiring or utterly insignificant. Ultimately you do not know yourself what kind of indirect influence nature has on your work, when you feel yourself part of it to such a large extent. Like many other things in life, nature can awaken feelings, and these feelings can have an influence on the music you write. But at the very time I am writing music, I must, intellectually speaking, turn my back on 'physical' nature and, for that matter, on everything but the piece I am working on. I must disregard various sundry feelings and distracting thoughts, which will only take attention away from the music that for the moment is the focal point demanding my full resources.

Working Conditions

There is, at any rate, scarcely any reason here to go into the many diverse feelings which may arise as the music is being written – feelings which are far from always in keeping with the music's bearing and character, and which therefore can be disturbing and as far as possible must be ignored or pushed right out of the mind. One can be nearly dizzy with fatigue, only half awake, hardly able to think a logical thought, and yet be able to compose, even work on a very complicated score. One can be possessed by an indeterminate horror of some unknown thing that has emerged from the subconscious, or be full of a sunny, liberating happiness, and yet continue working on music of a quite different character. As it is, I go to my work fresh every morning, with an inner joy and sense of anticipation with regard to what is to occur that day. Composing has become a necessity of life, an internal requirement in line with eating and sleeping, and if I am impeded by extraneous causes, I become all too easily restless, nervous and unreasonable.

Thus a fixed time for work is a wholly natural thing. If you are not particularly in the mood at the outset, you soon get into it through work. Sometimes, of course, there may be a noticeable disinclination to get started. But in that case you have learned to wait and, if it is practicably possible, to avoid any forcing of work, since forcing can never produce good results. You have learned to calm down your mind with less demanding tasks, such as adjusting notes, drawing bar-lines or, perhaps, orchestrating a movement. I orchestrate a composition in broad outline while I write the music, but as a rule I am content merely to indicate the desired instruments and combinations. The remaining task is to some extent a matter of calculating possibilities of sonority and requirements of balance; and those problems may be solved almost as you solve a cryptic crossword: you experiment, cross out, change, correct until the various factors are adjusted to one another in the only possible way.

Once a work is at last complete, it must be pushed right out of your consciousness; this is necessary if there is to be space for something new. How much has settled, how much drifts over into the more unconscious layers of the mind, you are not quite sure of when coming out of the magical circle that was created around the work while it was being written. You have learned things of various kinds, as much musical as psychological. But if there must be work later on with the composition – fixing little things after the first performance or making corrections before publication – you will invariably come to the music from the outside. To be sure, you can once again get into the piece and its spirit, but you come only as a guest.

Something similar may occur if one day you happen to hear a piece of music which was written perhaps decades earlier and which you think still has some validity. Then it may happen that you pull out the score with a view to eliminating some technical errors which are now thought embarrassing and which could easily have been avoided.

But that is a dangerous business to start, because you are a different person from the one who wrote the music. In individual cases you can perhaps enter into the spirit of an older composition, but it will always be as a guest that you come to the music, and even little technical alterations may affect the work and make its bearing insecure.

The Unconscious, Inspirational and Intellectual Processes

I shall now try to recapitulate, or generalise and further illuminate these fragmentary personal glimpses of creative work in music, with the continued understanding, of course, that these reflections, too, are tied to the recollection of purely subjective impressions and events.

As far as I can tell, three phases or layers may usually be found in all creative activity. They can hardly be distinguished in practice, because they are often so close in time that they become one interwoven force, although the individual layers will still be recognisable.

The first phase is so universally human that in itself it is not specific to, or only to be observed in, art, although it is probably a precondition for all true artistic creation.

It is unconscious and may be experienced as a spontaneous eruption in the mind, a flash or a state that can leave behind a strange, sometimes overwhelming feeling of bliss. Nothing else need take place. You can continue with your work, go on with your walk, or resume the reading of your book; but you know something important occurred at the moment when your mind was completely open and when you forgot about all concrete problems. You know that you had an experience outside time and place, outside your usual consciousness. Afterwards, perhaps, you are a bit troubled as well, for what was it that really occurred?

The only way open to approach this unknown is to look deeper within the human mind, and for good reason it can be only in your own mind, if you want to have first-hand knowledge of it. And with all the reservations inherent in being subject and object at the same time, you are compelled to search your mind in order to reach the cause of the experience. You must reject technical knowledge, experience and aptitude, must reject intellect and emotion, since none of these attributes, which are so significant for the creation of a work of art, may be said to be the actual cause.

Here you stand, then, in front of a closed door, a realm outside the reach of thought but which you feel is real, a realm about which it is hopeless to talk directly, hopeless to want to describe with words or to analyse, namely, the so-called *unconscious* in human beings.

Psychologists and psychiatrists are both involved with this realm, especially with people who are sick or have difficult mental conflicts. A number of often divergent theories, based on clinical experiments, have been proposed both about the individual and the collective unconscious and about its relationship to consciousness. But here it is a matter of an obviously positive force in people which I neither can nor want to try to describe and define, and in the face of which I must thus come to a halt; for no psychoanalytical terminology has been able, at least until now, to help the understanding of it, and every verbal formulation will constantly lead to wrong conclusions or away onto side-tracks. And yet I do not have any doubt about the reality of this source of energy and its tremendous importance for humans.

The encounter with the unconscious and creative force may sometimes have immediate consequences and be the direct cause of active work; in other cases it is preserved only as a memory in the mind. For the person who can produce artistic formulations, such an encounter will be able to elicit results which come we are talking about the second phase.

This second phase may be described as a short circuit between the first eruption and a point of catalytic action, which can release latent energy, and results in precisely what is often called *inspiration*. I have mentioned this occasionally abused term several times. The word, which in truth means 'breathing in', was extended long ago to mean 'being carried away' and 'suggestion from the divine'.

I shall leave the abuses out of consideration, since they are of no interest in this connection. But it is hardly an abuse of the word to say that a person can be inspired by a concrete event: the thrill of a distinctive and previously unknown landscape, the company of a person of whom you are fond, a heated discussion, an artistic experience, or any mental stimulus capable of setting a person's mind in motion.

These concrete occurrences are, many think, examples of the very fount of inspiration, its true cause, without which nothing will come about. This is *not* so, because they are examples only of subjective events able at a given instant to awaken something unknown and hitherto unconscious in the person, something which was perhaps experienced earlier without having produced direct artistic results. An inspiring event does not have to be significant in itself. It may even be without the slightest real interest or only a link in an artistic working process. But it is a contact with the unconscious and will effect a liberating release. The situation sets something in motion which for an artist means activation in an artistic medium, means that strong inner forces are pushing for action. What you happen to be busy with you must leave, so as to seek out a formulation of the *something* which is intruding, whether it is with words, notes, colours, or shapes, or – outside art – in science, politics or in apparently common, everyday doings.

Everyone can be inspired in this way, regardless of what they happen to be concerned with, because that life-giving force which grows out of experiencing things requires no specific medium. Potential artistic opportunities arise or are stimulated in these flashes or states, and at the same time you have – perhaps without being aware of it – learned something about space and time: you are suddenly able to perceive a long sequence of events merely by latching on to a rather small detail. You perceive that things stand still and yet at the same time are in motion, because in one breath you have grasped the simultaneity of part and whole.

Even after the first active efforts, inspiration can have an effect, be replenished, and solve potential problems, or in any case cast light on them in the intervals between work sessions, indeed, even during sleep. But above all, there is a demand in the inspiring experience that it come to fruition in some kind of material and that in some way it take shape, gain substance, and become alive.

The third phase is wholly conscious, but closely tied to the first two and with needs no lesser than those facing you in the rst two phases.

The need here is for fantasy, for the ability to imagine continuity and form, and – since our concern here is music – the existence of sound in acoustic reality. The composer must have a special sense for sonority, melody and rhythmic elaboration and, not least, the overall ability to think musically. It is in this stage that the formative and critical assessment of the material and its possibilities must take place. This is an absolute necessity if a major piece of music is to be realised satisfactorily.

The many, maybe scattered details must now be fused together into the total vision which, consciously or unconsciously, must already exist in the composer's mind. Sometimes it may seem that the details are arranged by themselves, that the material has an independent will to seek and find the right context and totality. But that is only a way of saying that the unconscious has a strong influence on the intellectual process, where factors like talent, experience, skill, desire, and many others are prominent.

To narrow down my reflections on the creative processes, I shall assert that the first phase, the experiencing of the unconscious and of the totality of things, is not a mystical condition, although it can be neither described nor analysed with sufficient clarity. It is often felt to be a gift of grace, in that it cannot be brought about by conscious effort or intellectual enterprise but is subject to the mind's openness and receptivity. It is undoubtedly a possibility for all human beings and is thus archetypical in its nature.

A pseudo-experience of similar character can be brought about through the artificial creation of ecstasy or with the aid of euphoriant drugs. The similarity may cause confusion, but the difference is very important. While the genuine experience fills and awakens *the whole person*, makes the mind ripe and engenders an active creative state, the artificially generated experience is passive, without a human background, a partial state with fortuitous effects.

Of the second phase – inspiration – there are, as I have said, numerous misunderstandings, especially about cause and effect, and chance and intention. It can really be described only in images derived from the possibly chance occurrence that triggered the initial experience.

Only with the third phase do we stand on firm ground. Here we have a realm accessible to the intellect, describable, characterised by conscious working with the material and by a considerable amount of time and work compared with the more obscure and often more transient unconscious and inspiring states which (or rather the parts of them that reach the light of day and may be traced by the intellect) absorb only a tiny fraction of the time required to create the ultimate work of art. This quantitative predominance accounts for conscious work with the material being made the subject of detailed examinations and descriptions, and for researchers and critics, as well as artists themselves, often considering the intellectual working process the most essential in all creative work. Thus it is said: 'Art is 1% inspiration and 99% perspiration' and 'Talent is work, and genius is still more work' – as elegantly said as true. But such a numerical statement contains only a part of the truth, for inspiration without work certainly has no artistic value, and persistent and prolonged work alone cannot create a work of art.

Furthermore, cause and effect in music cannot be established with certainty by analysis either of the work or of the working process. Thus we are again confronted with a complementary relationship, in that the unconscious creative state and intellectual analysis are mutually exclusive.

Second Movement
THE PERFORMER

One's Own Music

The immediate joy a person can have in listening to a single tone which he or she has produced – by singing or by playing – must be very ancient. The mere touching of a piano key, flick on a glass, blowing into a hollow tube may be a child's first encounter with something that was not there before, something the child itself has created and which can be the first step towards music.

The tone which people discover, and which they themselves produce and then listen to, places them in the ideal position to be creator, executant and listener all in one. We may perhaps be allowed to imagine that this is something which must have arisen before music existed for humanity, before it could be used for ritual purposes, for the accompaniment of words, for entertainment, dancing or performance. Humanity must have discovered musical sound before all these objectives could be realised.

There is no need here to delve into the many theories that exist about the origin of music: whether it is the individual's own voice or language, whether it is the rhythm in nature or in work, whether it is sounds created by people or given in nature, whether it is magic and invocation which could be the first cause. I will note here only that regardless of how humanity came into active contact with music, and regardless of the fact that this ideal situation always exists (where creator, executant and listener are one), specialisation has since evolved. Composers may play their own compositions on an instrument or sing them, and thereby be this trinity of creator, executant and listener; but if their music requires several instruments, they must subordinate themselves to the whole, or perhaps step back completely and hand over their place to other performers. Under such circumstances, which are quite normal today, a number of problems arise. How shall the music be performed? Can the notation give such precise information that there is only one way to play a work? Is a note-perfect rendition absolutely necessary, or can there be a certain leeway for the practising musician? Can performers allow themselves to display their own temperament, their particular technique and personal skill without betraying the composer's intentions and doing violence to the integrity of the work?

These questions lead directly to a discussion of the form of existence of the musical work, whether it is complete when the composer has written the last note, and whether its existence can be threatened by being performed – in other words, a discussion of its identity and integrity.

The Performance of Music

Like other composers, I have an ideal conception of the work I have written, of its character, its form, sound, dynamics and tempos. Since I rarely write a piece of music which leaves its realisation entirely to the improvisation of the performers (which some composers do), it has for me an identity, a character and a bearing which are quite specific for that particular work.

I know too (and have often learned) that it is particularly true that a large-scale work for orchestra can be performed only rarely according to my intentions at a first performance. This is always an unpleasant disappointment, but is basically something quite natural. The work, its spirit, ambience and shaping are, for good reason, unknown to the executants. There is not usually enough rehearsal time for close identification with the new piece, so the performers cannot rely on their instinct, let themselves go and play away, but must follow the notes more mechanically than is desirable. From this there can be a note-perfect rendition which is correct, but no real re-creation of the music – which is unsatisfactory to all concerned.

When I have not created a piece of music which through lack of knowledge, experience or technique is thoroughly unrealisable, and when the performers have the opportunity of coming to grips with it both technically and artistically, then the problems – if they have not lapsed – are nevertheless generally so clear that they can be solved.

A piece of music paper with a score on it consists of a series of signs and instructions for playing music that has been imagined.

These notes and signs can indicate pitch and loudness, phrasing and dynamics, timbre and tempo, but they cannot indicate every detail visually. The length of a bowing stroke, quality of a voice, width of a vibrato and dynamics of a phrase cannot be described precisely but only approximately. The note-signs can be supplemented with a mass of details and minute instructions to make the composer's intentions clearer; but however exact and detailed the score, it is still only a matter of a description of *possibilities*, which come about only when the music is realised in sound.

Now it is common knowledge that there are composers who want their music performed as precisely as possible, lest it become the victim of misinterpretation or outrageous distortion. This attitude can lead to the desire for a definitive rendition, fixed once and for all, which today can be realised with a recording, electronically, or with concrete, predetermined sounds on tape. But unless the music is written directly for electrical or mechanical devices and thus achieves meaning only through these media, the result will quickly become boring and dismal. Indeed, in particular cases it will have an embarrassing or a tragi-comic effect. Anyone who has heard a piece by Chopin played by an electric piano, where the performance is produced by means of a machine, knows what I mean. One needs only to compare it with a Rubinstein rendition to understand that it is not sufficient for the notes to be played in correct tempo and degree of intensity.

A piece of music, performed by musicians, *cannot* be represented exactly the same way each time it is performed, and there are many reasons why it has to be so: the degree of spirit in the performers, the influence of the audience in the hall, and the changing acoustic conditions (to mention only a few psychological and physical causes). Above all, and partly for these reasons, the performers must necessarily have some scope for movement if they are to respond to the demands placed on them. A performer, just like a composer, is a person with human emotions and an artist with artistic intentions, which may and must be realised in relation to the work that is to be performed. In addition, the player's or singer's position is always acute: there is no place for mistakes and corrections; they must do their best *here and now*! The extent of agreement between composer and executant is crucial for a successful result, for once any technical problems are solved, everything depends on to what extent the performer succeeds in representing the composer's intentions, in releasing the powers latent in the music.

An absolutely note-perfect rendition of a piece of music is in a sense an impossibility, because the note is a sign which does not have any quality by itself but gains it only through the playing of the performer.

The note may be set free by the executant who animates it through the sound, whether through bowing, blowing, striking or singing. And this animated sound has not just one single quality, but consists of an extremely large number of vibrations, of rhythmic, dynamic and timbral nuances, which are under the control of the intellect only in part. If the sound with all these countless impulses and indefinable nuances does not come alive, there will be no possibility that the piece of music comes alive as a whole. It must thus be acknowledged that, no matter whether the work to be performed is fairly familiar and has been tested over the years, the performer cannot repeat in all details what has been worked out at some earlier time. If this could occur, regardless of whether the technical aspect were objectively satisfactory, the result would become routine, stiff and mechanical, and would end up lacking richness or life.

The foundation of the presentation of the music can and must, of course, be based on established considerations or practices concerning the character of the music. But the result can be successful only if the performer is able to recreate the work anew every time. If this occurs, the executant is in the same position as the composer was when the work was written, since now the performer must similarly rely on instinct and intuition as well as technique and formative ability; which means that the unconscious powers must work in the same way as for the composer, if the result is to become something more than dull routine, pure and simple. Each player and singer must therefore have a certain freedom in presenting each piece, and consequently each piece of music must have a certain margin for interpretation, a scope for movement on the part of the executant.

Interpretation and Re-creation

The composer has responsibility for the quality of the music, its character and form, while the conductor of an orchestra or choir has responsibility for the realisation of the work, its shaping and progress.

When both parties know their craft, and when the conductor has mastered the work and can identify with it with conviction, it is my experience that a composer must intervene as little as possible at the rehearsals. This is partly because the notes say so much to skillful conductors that they form an impression of the music beforehand and of any potential problems in it; and so over-zealous intervention can easily cause confusion and insecurity. Then again the composer cannot fully evaluate many details of the performance in context until the music is heard in an unbroken whole, which as a rule occurs only at the final rehearsal – and then it is too late to raise objections. Ultimately one must give the conductor this freedom of interpretation if the result is to be convincing. A few examples may perhaps say something about these matters.

A few years ago a Russian conductor was going to perform one of my large-scale orchestral works, and I spoke with him shortly before the rehearsals were to begin. He asked me if he might take the music a little more slowly than prescribed, since he felt that would make it more expressive. I went along with that, because a refusal under those circumstances would only have made him unsettled.

It became some other work than the one I had imagined, over ten minutes longer, but performed with a conviction and insightful understanding which definitely lay within that margin that each piece of music must have.[1]

Another time on the radio I heard an Austrian conductor perform one of my symphonies in Vienna. At the time he was completely unknown to me, so I had not had the slightest contact with him. But his interpretation became a very positive experience. He obviously understood everything that I wanted with the music and shaped the many details into just that totality which

---

[1] [The work in question is *Epilog*, Op. 80 (1961–62), which in the performance referred to was about 40% longer than it would have been had the tempo indications in the score been taken literally.]

I had imagined when I wrote the work. It proved to be another confirmation that notes can be turned into music without any other explanation.[2]

It is no secret that a composer may often have an experience which is completely the opposite. Hence it is not only natural but also almost invariably necessary that composer and conductor exchange views before the performance. Then they can come in advance to an understanding and sort out the technical problems which otherwise could get in the way of a proper interpretation.

Whether one thinks about it or not, every performance of a piece of music will be an interpretation. But there are of course certain limits, even if they cannot be determined analytically and drawn up with a ruler. A casual performance will sound negative, as will an 'interesting' over-interpretation, because both show a lack of respect, understanding and insight. In both cases a limit has been exceeded. Very often there is a very thin dividing line between an acceptable interpretation and an executant's self-asserting, perhaps self-glorifying display, or, on the other side, between an acceptable interpretation and an impersonal and lacklustre 'objectivity'.

All in all, the performer's understanding of the work is an essential precondition for an artistically satisfying result. A true musician will never succumb to the temptation of showing off by over-interpreting but will have the artistic humility which opens up a deeper understanding and which determines a release of the sense of being at one with the music to be played or sung.

For many reasons, stylistic as well as psychological, problems can arise to make sympathy with the music difficult or quite impossible. But even in such unusual and extreme cases it may be said that the closer a musician comes to the essentials, to the shaping and the expressive force in the music to be performed, the greater is the artistic experience he or she can provide.

It is the performer who must implement the composer's musical ideas and intention; and since the music must be realised anew from the beginning every time it is performed, we must say that the true musician's interpretation is not merely a reproduction of the work, but a true re-creation.

[2] [In this case the composition was Chamber Symphony No. 1, Op. 53 (1951), and the conductor Herbert Häfner (1905–1952).]

Third Movement
THE LISTENER

The Effects of Music

Music is composed, performed and listened to; but what does music mean to the person who listens?

A long line of composers, psychologists, philosophers and poets has over the course of time made a detailed study of these matters. But there is deep disagreement among the many experts who have expressed themselves on the nature of music, its substance and its possibilites of providing an artistic experience. Professional and human presumptions may diverge, the artistic views of an era may have an influence, and observations may have too narrow a perspective. I shall therefore be content to give here a few glimpses of the variety in points of view by citing a number of short passages from important people from many centuries and many cultural epochs.

Quotations about Music

Johann Georg Sulzer (1720-1779)[1] writes that music is the art for expressing our passions through sounds. This is expanded by Wagner to: what music says is eternal, infinite and ideal. It does not speak of this or that person's passion, love or longing, but of passion, love, longing itself.

Beethoven remarks in one place that music is a higher revelation than all science and philosophy. This is carried further by Wilhelm Heinrich Wackenroder (1773-1798)[2] who, like many others, held that music begins where words stop, an opinion reinforced by the German writer Johann Ludwig Tieck

---

[1] [German philosopher who considered beauty in art a moral force capable of leading to ethical wisdom.]

[2] [An early German Romantic writer who was especially interested in the links between music and religion.]

(1773–1853),[3] for whom music is faith's last mystery, the revealed religion.

Others have a somewhat different view of music: thus, for example, Théophile Gautier (1811–1872),[4] who notes that music is the most unpleasant and for many people the most beloved form of noise; Democritus (ca. 460–ca. 370 B.C.), for whom music is a luxury without deeper significance; or Immanuel Kant (1724–1804), who places music lowest on the artistic ladder, because it is only a plaything of feelings which gives no substance for reflection.

For Plato (ca. 427–ca. 348 B.C.), on the other hand, music has an essential ethical significance, since it has the ability to express moral qualities and is not just a means for unthinking enjoyment. K'ung-Fu-Tzu[5] (551–479 B.C.) expresses it thus: if a person lacks those virtues which belong to humanity, then why does such a person have anything to do with music?

Among poets there is in general more agreement. Molière writes, among other things, that if everyone learned music, the way would be open to compromise and to the supremacy of peace over the whole world. Shakespeare touches on the same line of thought when he has one of his characters say that no one should trust the man who does not have music in himself or who is not moved by its sweet sound.

Eduard Hanslick (1825–1904)[6] speaks more rationally of music's independent values when he claims that the beauty of a piece of music is specifically musical, and that its content is forms moved in sound.

With extreme rationalism, William James (1842–1910) equates seasickness and music, which for him is merely an incidental peculiarity of the nervous system without purposeful significance,

---

[3] [A prolific early German Romantic writer, known for his tales of the bizarre and fantastic, and for his later historical realism.]

[4] [The French Romantic writer who was deeply concerned with spiritual ideas of beauty which would transcend perception of it.]

[5] [Better known as Confucius.]

[6] [German aesthetician, supporter of Schumann and Brahms and critic of Wagner and Bruckner; he considered the meaning of music to be formal and abstract, as Holmboe's discussion suggests.]

in complete contradistinction to Frank Howes (1981–1974),[7] who writes that music is a form of knowledge, or Susanne K. Langer (1895–1985), who stresses[8] that music is not communication; it is insight that is music's gift, because it gives emotional satisfaction, intellectual confidence, and musical understanding.

This excursion into the thoughts of others probably does not clarify the problems but rather shows that music may be pondered from extremely different viewpoints, and that there are always new considerations to be taken into account. I shall therefore continue to discuss the relationship between humanity and music and attempt to delve further into the many uncertainties and problems that draw a veil over music and its significance for humanity.

Comprehension of Music

As I have said, a piece of music truly exists only when it is heard, because its emotional content, artistic qualities and form cannot be revealed and come alive until the music is displayed in the dimension of time. Just as an architectural drawing is not a house, and a script not a film, so a sheaf of pages of music manuscript is not music.

To be sure, music can be written down on manuscript paper and thereby be made the object of reproduction and analysis. But that will only mean that, through a series of different signs and conventional instructions, the composer is giving information about the pitch, duration and intensity of the notes, their relation to one another, and about the means employed in the particular work.

Thus music which is written down exists only as a *possibility*, and it achieves reality only when the signs are converted into sound or the imagining of sound. Music must either be sensed directly or be 'heard' with the inner ear in order to be able to reveal itself and become alive for the listener.

[7] [A music critic on *The Times* from 1925 to 1960; his books include studies of Vaughan Williams and Walton.]

[8] [In *Philosophy in a New Key*, Harvard University Press, Cambridge (Mass.), 1942.]

Like many other listeners, I have often found that a piece
of music can have different effects on me each time I hear it.
Now I am normally an attentive listener and often am already
familiar with the work being performed or its style, so the cause
may be the variable quality of performance. With an unsatisfactory performance it may happen that the work, despite all
one's attentiveness, will not open up – perhaps because essential motives are drowned in the general orchestral tumult; or
because poor intonation has a painfully disturbing and distracting effect; or because wrong tempi completely upset all
the relationships and proportions. All this can give such a distorted impression of the music that its substance and meaning
are missed entirely.

It is, of course, obvious when this happens. You experience
nothing, or only a caricature, because an incompetent or
indifferent performance is not able to recreate the work as the
composer will have imagined it. But that is not an adequate answer, because exactly the same thing may occur if, let us say,
you attend a private gathering to listen to tapes or records. It
may be a matter of a new, unknown work or a specific performance of a work you already know and you may now have the
opportunity to hear the music after the lapse of a week or a
month. In this case both the work and the performance are, of
course, absolutely identical from one time to the next.

On such occasions you disregard as far as is possible the unavoidable acoustical deficiencies and concentrate on the music
itself. For example, I first heard Stravinsky's *Symphony of Psalms*
at a gathering where everyone was interested in getting acquaint-
ed with the composition, which was then unknown to us. And
I recall how great an experience it was to listen to this powerful
music, and how alive the music was in my memory afterwards.
But some time later I heard the same record under the same
conditions but in the company of different people. There was
a distinct difference in the attentiveness of the gathering, and
several of the people present were obviously uninterested, because little restless movements and sounds, which would not
usually be distracting, gave the atmosphere in the room a mark
of restlessness and restrained impatience, which in this instance
closed off any direct experience of the work. As for myself, the
music faded, even if only for a time; for me, as for some others

who were there, it was killed, and they had to admit their disappointment with it.[9]

Emotional contagion of that sort is not rare. It is negative and, momentarily, can disturb or destroy the artistic impact because it has destroyed the possibility of catching hold of and experiencing the music being heard. Yet the situation may just as often be positive, as anyone who is connected with music knows. It may happen that well-known music which has not meant anything before may suddenly admit of unknown qualities, without any causes being detected other than that those around may have a positive attitude and one's own receptivity may be heightened.

Here is another experience among many that are comparable. As a boy I heard Schubert's B minor Symphony, 'The Unfinished', on a record, and it made a deep impression on me. Over time, however, the music lost its power and no longer could affect my mind, not even in excellent performances in the concert hall. I had 'grown out of it' – an experience I know many people have undergone with all kinds of music, and which others will certainly undergo again and again. Many years later I happened to hear the old record once more, and, as on the first occasion, I was alone. And then the work opened up for me again in all its unfathomable richness and beauty. I re-experienced it with a new understanding – and fortunately it has been like that ever since.

I shall not explore here the psychological causes of these different experiences, which are usually quite simple, but sometimes undoubtedly complicated. I will mention only what they have proved to me that music belongs to the individual who listens to it, and that it does not live until it can reveal its hidden energies and be received by a human mind. And further, that the listener's opinion of a piece of music cannot be an absolute criterion for its quality, since both receptivity and attitude towards a work may be quite variable and may easily be influenced by extraneous causes, without our always being aware of it.

Muzak and Entertainment

It is probably true that most people have a passive relationship to music and expect and want it only as a sort of sonic furnishing

---

[9] [The essay on pp. 117–21 discusses the *Symphony of Psalms* further.]

supposed to fill up an unbearable emptiness outside oneself and hide an uncomfortable emptiness inside, or supply a nerve-calming background for other activities. Thus music, in a manner of speaking, decorates the air without forcing itself on our attention. It should not be taken in but should nonetheless be there.

In department stores, in offices, indeed, even in homes, radio or tape recordings can while away the whole day with perfunctory strains known as 'muzak', which usually has little to do with real music, and which merely fills a void, with the side-effect of closing the door on real musical impressions. 'Muzak' is negative in its effect because it blocks the mind and prevents people from listening and developing their receptivity. And this effect reaches far beyond the realm of music. There is 'muzak' put out on tapes which play continuously; and there would be no reason to waste many words on the subject in this connection were it not that the dividing line is so vague between sonic wallpaper and the immensely large area called 'light music' or 'pop music'.

Music whose only purpose is entertainment may have somewhat the same function as sonic furnishing, even if there can be significant differences in quality. But light music can in addition give comfort, create good spirits, amuse and delight. It has its effects only in the present and is normally quickly forgotten, because it is still only a rather convenient background for other activities. It may have specific functions (to increase the impact of a film, play or the text of a folksong); it can comfort and amuse; and it can be linked with associations or with personal experiences – remembrance of a Christmas holiday, a first encounter, falling in love – and thus take on a certain indirect value for the individual involved.

Much good music has been written over the years with the aim of entertaining without obtruding, and much important music has been used for the same ends. We are familiar with dinner music, divertimenti, ballads and film music from the last two or three centuries, music which in many cases is indistinguishable from music of similar quality, to be heard and understood exclusively on its own terms, and which therefore demands attention.

Undoubtedly, music always contains a certain amount of

entertainment and play. But for those who are more interested in music, entertainment pure and simple is not enough. They demand that the music have a standard that can both meet their emotional needs and satisfy their intellect. Music must be a challenge to their purely musical sense, their objective skill and their capacity for musical and human understanding.

The Specialised Background

The sharpening of abilities through specialised studies is, for creator and executant as much as for the listener, a good start on the best possible way to look for and find what is important in music, without being seduced by well-known technical niceties or getting lost in superfluous diverting associations.

Those who listen with their whole mind are capable of experiencing music directly, if we assume that well-informed people can disregard their particular knowledge at the moment of performance.

The difficulties the specially trained person can encounter arise not because knowledge, ability and discipline are in themselves hindrances. But this knowledge, instead of being a means to a deeper understanding, may become self-sufficient, become an end in itself and thus a deadweight that can encumber a skilled perception of the music and make it slanted and one-sided.

In extremely unfavourable instances, alas not at all rare, the expert can be a bad listener. The violinist will listen with interest to a violin concerto but notice less the musical continuity than the soloist's playing and technique. Similarly, the composer will be inclined to concentrate exclusively on style and technique when a new composition is performed, and will therefore miss any general musical qualities there may be in the work. The theorist will try to dissect what is heard and fit the parts of the music into purely theoretical boxes. The critic will, even while listening, consider the formulation of what is heard in a suitable linguistic mode. In all these ways the result may possibly add up to thorough specialised knowledge, but musically it will be barren, because attention will be directed towards the technical, formal or stylistic qualities – which can certainly produce joy or disappointment, admiration or indignation, but no true musical experience.

The Emotional Stimulus

On the other hand, specialised knowledge plays a lesser role for many music lovers who may have learned something about music, and possibly have learned an instrument or sung in a choir. But whether they can play or sing does not really matter, because the crucial thing for them is only the effect of the music on their mind, whether it pleases them and whether they come to feel something in listening. There may be considerable differences between what any one of them gets out of the music, and many will be able to follow the course of the music only to a certain extent, since there may be long periods when the music slips by unnoticed before the listener is aroused anew, affected emotionally by distinctive details, by dynamic tensions or climaxes, or by things that are melodically beautiful. Music gives them the opportunity to release latent or repressed feelings, and they are thus not at all as passive as those listeners who look exclusively for entertainment. On the other hand they are able to follow music only insofar as it fills an emotional need or awakens a hidden reserve of feeling.

The emotional experience may be violent or gentle, invigorating or soothing, each according to how the character and progress of the work are felt and comprehended by the listeners. They can be spellbound and dizzied by an orchestra's turbulent orgies of sound, thrilled by a soloist's charming tone or virtuosic brilliance. But above all music attracts them because it can liberate their pictorial fantasy and set their minds in motion. What images, fantasies and colour projections a particular person creates is an individual matter and may vary considerably from person to person. But for all of these people music becomes a source of energy that releases private feelings and dream images, most often with no connection, or only a superficial one, with the music that is heard.

Experimental Music

From the time of the Renaissance, when humanity put the sun and itself at the centre of its world picture, the delicate balance among composer, performer and listener has been severely shaken at regular intervals; and the situation recently has become heavily strained, not to say critical. The causes of fluctuation in musical developments are numerous. Here I shall mention only those important social changes, crucial technical inventions and very disparate relations to concepts like 'tradition' and 'quality' which have significant effects on the present situation.

Right up to the nineteenth century, innovation was a natural thing on all sides. Music was written, used and put away. The works of the fathers were looked upon as hopelessly old-fashioned and were forgotten. New music was required for every event, big or small, because there was a need for music suitable for sacred or secular purposes, with seldom any question of re-use. The music was valued chiefly for its utility and for the splendour it could add to the event. There was thus a tradition of innovation throughout history, with its source in a need, in new thinking, which met with both opposition and acclaim, of course, but which was not seen in a historical perspective.

The innovations of Romanticism signified a notable alteration of these conditions. Even before this, people had begun to enjoy music with no other purpose than to listen to it. The intrinsic value of music now became a revelation for many. A new interested public came into existence and the historical past became a living reality. The great historical composers – Haydn or Beethoven, for example – could not be avoided. Mozart was performed again, and occasionally discoveries went as far back as Bach and Palestrina. People dug even further back in the past and found a new beauty in old music, without knowing very much about the social and aesthetic conditions which then obtained.

Thus historical music was no longer historical. It became current on an abstract level. It became relevant, yet without any direct connection with contemporary problems. The tension between firm historical values and problematic contemporary endeavours helped eventually to produce confusion in the listener; and there arose a gap of understanding which was difficult to smooth out and overcome.

After the First World War, developments gathered distinct speed. The times were continually unsettled, politically and socially as much as culturally. Matters were in ferment everywhere, and musical life, too, was in revolt, with intense conflicts between customary, traditional ways and new standards of value. A faded post-Romanticism and a vehement expressionism were opposed by a reaction that swept away the antiquated and the uninhibited with sober, concrete and objective means. People were disillusioned after the War, wanted to get away from unreal dreams, from the self-centred – they wanted facts and a firm grip on matters. The orgies of sound made by monster orchestras and the strong passions had only led to disaster; so now there had to be a regaining of composure with clarity, simplicity, moderation and counterpoint. But one of the results of this development was the increased isolation of the sober young composers, a gulf between their endeavours and the wants and needs of the public, which were never markedly sober.

This alienation of the public from young, experimental music was increased further around and after the middle of this century. On one hand, tradition now has a stronger attraction for people than ever before, since, thanks to records, radio and tape recordings, we have easy access to classical music and its masterworks from practically every era, so that music from the eighteenth and nineteenth centuries is just as alive for people today as when it was newly created. On the other hand, developments have accelerated, so that there is no longer a generation between new ideas and ideals, nor even the familiar period of a decade. Stylistic trends come along at a rate that makes them seem to be treading on one another's toes in a mutual struggle to come to the fore. It has become a kind of neurotic obsession that only the new has value, that novelty must be valued more highly than quality.

In the thirties new objectivity, neo-Baroque and neo-Classicism, which were reactions to the monstrous and distended expansions of post-Romanticism, were abruptly interrupted by the Second World War, but continued afterwards in other guises: twelve-note music, totally predetermined and indeterminate music; with electronics, alternative music, new simplicity, collages; and a re-adoption of grandparents' ways of thinking with a slightly nostalgic neo-Romanticism, neo-Impressionism, neo-traditionalism, and many other ripples on the surface of developments.

The picture that appears of new music therefore becomes a twin portrait before us, somewhat simplified and generalised.

Young composers fight for their right to artistic independence, for freedom to feel their way, to experiment, and to find new paths. It is often a bitter fight against the habitual, against rigid tradition, and especially against the existing period's entrenched and tested ideas and what have become commonplace means. Their new ways of thinking often lead them far away from the established formal designs, because they must see things in fresh perspectives and turn everything upside-down, so as not to stagnate in facile imitation. Opposition increases the clash, and lack of sympathy and understanding in others has now created not just a rift but an abyss between people and their ability to understand one another.

Under these circumstances, the relationship between the creator and the listener becomes a vicious circle: modern and experimental works repel a large part of the public, so that these works are rarely performed in concerts and almost never repeated. Thus the possibility of familiarity is precluded, a familiarity which could lead to deeper understanding. The sad result is that the alienation persists.

The portrait of the 'modern' composer in every period is that of a pre-occupied person who finds the average listener slow, uninterested, disapproving and sometimes rancorous. If there can be said to be any contact at all between the parties, it is negative. Usually, the young react spontaneously and aggressively or with affected indifference when faced with the animosity of those around them. The situation is fairly constant, but not for the parties involved, since more fanatical young people add to the flow all the time, learn from the slightly older composers, and then reject them and their works in order to make room for their own fresh ideas and their own development; while the slightly older rebels mellow and acquire a new relationship with their colleagues or are forgotten.

The other side of the twin portrait is the band of listeners who are confronted once in a while with contemporary music on the radio or at a concert. Unprepared as they are for something new, they are distressed: what are they supposed to do with this unfamiliar and incomprehensible music? They are far less interested in encountering ideas and programme notes than in listening to music, and most often the music strikes them as destroying all their customary values. It can scarcely be a surprise that the reaction from the listener must also be negative. According to temperament, the result will vary from hesitant waiting, irritated dismissal and straight indignation to acid amusement or agitated anger. The many conflicting tendencies and isms only seem to be a superficial pretence of joy for the few, a neurotic reaction to certain catchwords from social and political developments, or an artificial transference to music of ideas and manners from other arts.

What lies behind these unfamiliar and therefore cacophonous sounds is rarely perceived as anything but destruction, because it is usually the *means* which are immediately repellent; it is the *way* things are expressed which is incomprehensible. And this blunt balking at these means is what prevents any insight for the unacquainted into the music itself and what precludes the perception of any possible musical substance or quality.

Conversely, today's untutored listeners immediately understand without aid the musical language of a Bach, Beethoven, Chopin, Verdi or Wagner, for all that there are quite significant differences in these composers' ways of expressing themselves and in their means; and they were often severely attacked in their own time for incomprehensibility. Listeners today may have widely divergent tastes and have their preferred favourite composers among the older ones, but an attitude, positive or negative, depends here not so much on the very different means (which are all known through countless performances) as on the nature of the artistic statement, of the musical substance.

Whereas the attitude to the new forms of music very easily stiffens into a static negativeness and aloofness for those indifferent to and unacquainted with them, it is somewhat different for those with prior interest. They want to know something about what is actually happening in contemporary music, and will gladly make the effort to get to know the background. Thus they hunt out experimental music in the few places where it is performed.

Their prior interest may be rooted in a common human desire to broaden their musical horizons, or it may be a result of intellectual curiosity, which is why they study statements and programme notes in an attempt to understand the music by these verbal explanations and elucidations. Or they may have an especial interest in all things in contemporary life and thus try, through the various tendencies in music, often mutually struggling as they are, to discover why and how things occur.

They have or obtain an insight into the new directions and ideas; they can participate in the continuing discussion and contribute their points of view on a relatively professional level if artistic controversies should arise.

With some people, the background to their interest may be a delight in the variety of music, in its possibilities of expression being realisable in constantly new ways. With others, the interest may be due to a fear of not being 'with it' (the same fear that a slightly older composer may feel), or to a snobbery for what is new solely because it is new, regardless of whether it is understood or not.

A few words about this last – snobbery – may be in order here.

Snobbery

A snob comes and listens to experimental music only when and where it is fashionable, where it is 'in' to be interested in it. That is why snobbery is a far more common phenomenon with classical music, where the rubbish has been filtered out over the course of the years so that only the fruitful material is left.[10] This gives snobs a convenient security, so they can allow themselves to express their admiration for music which they neither understand nor really have any interest in.

The snob's problem is not musical but social, in one form or another. Vanity, social climbing, adjustment or habit are most often the forces driving the snob to have anything at all to do with music. There is no contact, no connection between the snob and the music to be heard in a concert hall. The music is a troublesome detail and an unfortunate necessity, if the snob wants to turn up in the 'right' places and have the possibility of meeting the 'right' people.

The negative side of this is obvious, not least because the snob's insensitivity to music and artistic indifference create all too often an attitude to artistic qualities which appears distorted and negative.

But there is also a positive side. For one thing, the unavoidable

---

[10] [Even if the music of the past which is still performed is (mostly) good, it does not follow that music rarely or never performed is worse. There are numerous examples, Vagn Holmboe's included, which show that unfamiliar music may be as good as, or better than, a lot of music much more widely known.]

contact with music may in fortunate cases lead to the seed of understanding and evaluation. For another, snobbery is a very varied phenomenon. It ranges from a completely negative attitude to music to an indeterminate admiration, even veneration for beauty and skill. The border between ugly snobbery confronting something not understood and a ready willingness to understand is in any case uncertain and thus can not be brought out with clarity – which is why a blanket condemnation of all snobbery easily becomes rash and unfair.

Folk Music

There is a particular realm where the connections between human emotions, motor impulses and music come right out to the surface and thus become easier to observe – and that is folk music.

There is no intention here to go deeply into what is called folk music, neither into its variety of type and form, nor into its connection with European or other art music in general. Only a short sketch will be given here of those aspects which have particular interest for the relationship between human beings and music.

In folk music the intellectual element is quite unimportant, which is why this music is often of no interest to and is not appreciated by people with deep theoretical knowledge of and insight into music. But precisely because intellectual problems rarely or never arise, the fact is that this music in its innermost nature is emotional, that it releases universally human emotions, and that, with or without words, it is able to redeem human suffering, joy and longing, the human need to be with other people and for merriment and dance.

Folk music is usually anonymous. Only in rarer instances is a name linked to a special piece of music, often a dance which is a little out of the ordinary but which is accepted by the group. It is crucial that it is the wishes and needs of a group or an entire nation that are expressed by the individual, who can on the other hand formulate, create and perform the music as her or his entirely personal expression.

An artistically gifted person has the potential, within this framework, to be at once a catalyst for the whole group and at the same time to be able to present what is frequently a distinct artistic, even a virtuoso accomplishment. The artistic brilliance may be successful and sometimes amaze those around; but apart from the depth of the interest and admiration it awakens, it will always be the emotional side which is perceived by everyone as the essential and readily understandable thing that can move the sympathetic listener, because it is an expression formulated for everything that touches every single group (or the people).

A personal event, an unhappy love affair, a social injustice, indignation over political oppression or the unfettered joy of living and need for development achieve their spontaneous expression through the singing or playing of the individual. Others may take over the music, identify with its conceptions and possibilities, polish it, change and expand it according to other circumstances and needs, and thus gradually make it the inalienable spiritual property of an entire people – a living expression, never completely formulated, of this people's feelings, wishes and current existence. At the same time it is outwardly a manifestation, a testimony to the people's identity, a confirmation of its unique existence.

Media such as radio and television give many people today the opportunity to hear music which was once tied to limited regions and meant something there; for example, some country towns in the Balkans, a Flamenco grotto in Spain, a street in London or a cafe in inner Copenhagen.

The opportunities the media offer can promote understanding of foreign people and cultures, can give a glimpse of others' emotional lives and impressions of their circumstances. Something comparable can occur with unknown domestic tribal or folk music, which also flourishes, although in other milieux and in other forms than those generally known and accepted.

Valuable information may be obtained through radio talks that play examples of folk music from abroad. In addition, through their music deeper understanding may be obtained of the human and social backgrounds of foreign cultures.

But there is a negative side to this, namely, that music in the media tends to freeze at a random point in its otherwise unbroken development. The performance of a certain piece quickly becomes established as the only valid norm. The music is no longer worked at, and it is eventually accepted passively as a picturesque change from the familiar.

A foreign folk music may potentially be used for dancing and other entertainment; but even in that case there is rarely the possibility of understanding it properly within its own backgrounds, torn away as it is from its original milieu. It stagnates, and is most often reduced to a banal entertainment, which is soon forgotten. As with all other music that is reduced in this way, the possibilities for people to come into contact with the special qualities in the music are forfeit, music which, through its own apparent and concealed power, can make what is distant close and broaden human understanding.

This I shall explore more deeply in what follows.

Fourth Movement
THE INEXPLICABLE

Myth and the Experience of Ecstasy and Magic

Since the dawn of time humanity has known of the inexplicable power of music over people, indeed, over all of nature's creatures. We have known its effects, both good and bad; we have known that it can, with the strength of a natural force, cause men and women to forget themselves and their surroundings, that it can lead to frenzied actions; yet it is also capable of alleviating the pains of the mind and the body. Myths and legends tell of music's spontaneous effects on people's minds. These myths have hardly sprung up out of the blue but are undoubtedly poetic – stylised expressions for experiences over centuries.

Orpheus' playing of the lyre caused people and animals to become enthralled and carried away in listening; even trees and rocks moved from their places to follow the sound of his music. Odysseus had to have himself bound to the mast of a ship in order to be able to resist the Sirens' alluring tones. King Erik of Denmark went berserk, merely by listening, despite all warnings, to a minstrel's singing and playing.[1] And the folk ballad's Mr Villemand was able with his golden harp to save his bride from the cruel river-troll: 'he plucked his harp in wrath, and his bride from the arms of the ogre; he plucked his harp to the depths, and the ogre had to leave his shoal'.[2]

The myths say something important about the relationship of people to music and the power of music over people. And the lessons of later eras concur: song lightens the woe and torment of the mind, and it can make tired marching men forget their aching feet. Music can sometimes excite, sometimes pacify. It can actually compel people to physical expression, to dancing

[1] [King Erik Egode, who ruled from 1095 to 1103.]

[2] [This is a rather literal prose translation which is not intended to capture the earthy rhythms, rhymes or overall linguistic style of the original lines.]

or other action. But it may also dampen restlessness in the mind and open the way to quiet contemplation.

To cast a little more light on these matters, we must discuss subjects of a non-musical nature, mental states with which it is both difficult and problematic for a lay person to be involved. There are two phenomena of considerable psychological import, two particular states of mind both of which say something important in the relationship between music and people, namely, the *ecstatic* and the *magical*.

They are at once peripheral and central and are often the most extreme consequence of the psychological effect of music. Music can send people into ecstasy, in which condition they are unaware of their own egos. Or it can bring them to a magical state of mind, in which case the experience is so intense that they are oblivious of time and place.

According to its root meaning, *ecstasy* is a state in which one is outside oneself, is pulled away from one's ego, and the state may vary from rapturous enthusiasm, through frenzied intoxication, all the way to hysterical craziness. The word 'magic' stems from the Chaldean astrologers, the *Magi*, but over time has taken on more varied meanings than the merely astrological, so that magic may not only be sorcery (both black and white) but also a transforming power. Finally, the word may refer to something enchanting in the specifically artistic sense.

Both concepts have multifarious shades of meaning; as states they have a few things in common. They pull a person away from an everyday situation, overcome inhibitions, and open the mind to those experiences or adventures to which music can give entry, all according to its kind and nature. But there the similarity also ends, for whereas the ecstatic state, when extreme, is without ego-consciousness and often leads to physical expression, to dancing or unpremeditated action, in the magical state an awareness of what is going on in or around oneself – and not least of the music itself – is maintained, although also transformed.

I myself have experienced both states in connection with music, and in order to cast more light on them I shall now briefly recount two different episodes.

I have experienced the ecstatic in Romania, where many years ago I took part in the great round dance *Hora* (notably the one

On the Faroe Islands in 1978, with the conductor Ólavur Hátún
(photograph by Meta May Holmboe)

called *Ciuleandra*) in a mountain village.[3] The only thing that appeared to occur was that you joined the dance and tried to remember the dance's steps. But after a short time your state was completely altered. Details faded, everything around you became blurred, and gradually everything disappeared from your consciousness. Afterwards you were aware that you had lost your ego-consciousness and had become completely wrapped up in the collective of dancers, that the swirling music and rousing rhythm had compelled you to forget everything except becoming one with the circle.

I have experienced the magical in a similar way, oddly enough, and likewise in a round dance, namely the Faroese *Dansiringur*.[4] Here too you were transformed from being an isolated figure

---

[3] [*Hora* means essentially 'round dance', i.e., a dance performed in one or more moving circles. *Ciuleandra* has no precise translation.]

[4] [Again, this simply means 'round dance'.]

*Holmboe at Sibiu, Romania, in 1934, notating Romanian folk
dances from a group of musicians (lăutari).*

into becoming one with the collective of dancers, and you noticed
an absolutely magnetically connected sense of community with
the whole circle. But in comparison to the ecstatic dance, here
you were conscious of your ego. You could follow the song's
narrative and could yourself sing along in the refrain, as well
as you could manage.

Musically there is a big difference between the two events.
The Romanian music is instrumental, with vibrant and flutter-
ing tones that quickly fly by, and firm, extremely rousing
rhythms. It is music which I also gladly listen to without taking
part in the dance. But in that case it is felt – at least by me –
to be less ecstatic and more aesthetically interesting and musically abstract.

On the Faroes the dance is borne along solely by song; there
is never any use of instruments. The melody is powerfully
chiselled, worked over through centuries; the rhythm is heavy
and firm, almost a stamping on the ground. But if you hear the
song without doing the dancing, it may still retain a certain
symbolic-magical effect for a time, until, after the first twenty

or twenty-five stanzas, it becomes monotonous, unless you are able to follow the narrative of the song.[5]

I have also taken part in these dances without noticing anything but a quite conscious delight in dance and music, perhaps because I have not always been predisposed, and furthermore have as a rule had a professional interest and thus have been more an observer than a participant.

In Romania I have, for example, often been an observer in order to write down the music. Then I have observed how the participants in the Învîrtita,[6] the common opening dance of the mountainous regions, warm up. First the dancers stand completely motionless in many small circles. Then they begin to shake their whole bodies; their feet twitch, and the dancers move like sleep-walkers with their eyes closed, then gradually faster and faster until the circles whirl around amongst one another.

In these dances, as in all the others, music is of course a prerequisite for the state of mind but is neither the real cause of it nor an end in itself. The stirring, affective or simply rousing performance of the music is a necessary means, just as the physical movement is, and the close but not erotic contact between people in the circle of the dance.

Ecstasy related to music has many phases and degrees of strength, all the way from unconscious foot-tapping in time with music, up to more or less distinctly psychic, even psychotic states. But since music can largely stimulate bodily expression, the possibilities for the ecstatic which music gives are frequently realised through one of the many kinds of dance, varying with the frame of mind of those around and the general level of culture.

In the well-known dances for two, there is not uncommonly a trace of the ecstatic. The particular couple moves in a closed world, taken with either the delight of the dance and its movements, with the sensual contact with the partner, or – perhaps less frequently – with the rhythmically rousing music. The types of dances have changed with the times, but the effect on the dancers and the reactions of the rather narrow-minded

---

[5] [It is not unusual to find Faroese songs or dances with a hundred four-line stanzas, and there are some with three hundred or four hundred.]

[6] [This word means a 'turning dance'.]

have been conspicuously uniform over the years, especially each time a new kind of dance has received the full glare of publicity. This was true even for the famous Viennese waltz, which at the outset was disreputable and was looked upon as the height of indecency; but this did not prevent it from later being approved in all quarters, at the same time as its nature was changed somewhat: it was urbanised in the same way as nearly all the later dances, such as the tango; and rock, beat and many other, more recent kinds of dance music.

Dance music, the implicit or explicit aim of which is to stimulate to the point of excitement, to liberate to the point of abandon, reaches a culmination with the dionysiac expression in many dances marked by ritual. For example, dervishes use the euphoric effects of dance and music to attain the self-denying ecstasy for which they long and which for them, according to many reports, is a feeling of ego-oblivion and an ascent into the cosmos.

Ecstatic moments may similarly be observed in march music, in theatre music, orchestral music, and in the connection of music with words, as well as in many kinds of community singing, where the word and its meaning have particular significance and where the participants already have a certain religious, national or political outlook in common. Or in workers' songs and in the little reiterated cries like 'Heave ho' or 'Alley-oop', which can ease the effort when a heavy boat has to be hauled onto land. In all these cases we are talking about utility music in the broadest sense, i.e., music or song the purpose of which is not so much a furthering of musical experiences as to help provide mental relief or forgetting, and physical release. And to this end, music and song may be used to a certain extent to suspend the usual ego-consciousness in the participants and thereby cause them to forget any pressing personal difficulties.

Of course, ecstasy in the present context is interesting only in the musical side of the subject, and here the question arises as to which means can best be used to attain an ecstatic state.

It must be said at once that the wholly decisive factor is rhythm. Regardless of whether rhythm is tied up with lively and penetrating melodies, with whirling or insistent figurations, or – the complete opposite – with extremely primitive and very simple melodic formulas, ecstasy or ecstatic states will be reached through the rhythmic repetition, repetition, repetition. And the repetition

very soon acquires whatever aesthetic qualities are needed to
disappear from one's consciousness. What is left will be only the
dull or inflammatory, perpetually repeated rhythm that enters
the blood and affects the person.

Ecstasy quite definitely has deep psychological significance,
but nowhere near a corresponding musical interest. For
participants who seek the ecstatic, the music's potential aesthetic
qualities are immaterial, since they appreciate the music
exclusively for its ability to create a self-forgetting state and a
psychophysical release. For non-participants, i.e., people who have
kept their consciousness and reason and who therefore are in
a position to follow and register the music, this possibility of the
ecstatic will be absent, and interest in the artistic side of matters,
in whatever qualities the music may have, quickly disintegrates
in the presence of the endless rhythmic and melodic repetition,
which is soon sensed as a monotonous and boring emptiness.

The magic of music, its effect of enchantment on people, is
rather more difficult to isolate and describe. If the listener is
moved by its magical power, a purely physical result may possibly
come about: a shiver down the spine, a tingling in the scalp; but
there is nothing which demands bodily expression. On the
contrary! Here it is plain that other parts of the mind are touched
and activated, parts which are receptive to artistic impressions,
which are marked more by thought and emotion than by urges
and motion.

Thus the magical in music demands almost everywhere far
more of the listener than the ecstatic: not only a receptive state
of openness and a capacity for sympathetic understanding but
also – paradoxically enough – a mixture of relaxed calm and
intent listening. You are pulled away from your usual state, from
your daily problems; you forget time and place, experience
through music a new dimension of existence, and thereby have
the capacity to come to an insight that would otherwise have been
closed to you. You are transformed, enriched and strengthened
by the encounter with a reality different from the familiar
everyday kind but equally real.

The two states discussed are present in all musical experience,
but in varying degrees of strength, intensity and mutual blend.
Whereas music with a decided emphasis on the ecstatic is most
often out of the ear and scarcely remembered once the self-

forgetting intoxication is over, the effect of the magical can live in the mind long after the actual impact and sometimes even gain permanent value. Here the state of consciousness is admittedly transformed, but the intellect has not been out of action. On the contrary, it has been sharpened and is thus able to remember all the impressions and to keep them alive in the mind. It may therefore be said that a moment of magic enters into all ideal listening to music.

Before I go into this particular phenomenon – ideal listening – we must discuss the significance of memory for musical understanding and also look for an approach to such indefinable concepts as quality, substance and the experiencing of music.

Memory and Recognition

The ability to remember what has been perceived is an important condition for the comprehension of all art. For music this ability is not just important but an absolute necessity.

A painting or a sculpture can be taken in directly and immediately. Attention may, either guided by the artist's intentions or quite independently, move amongst the individual parts of the work and compare tensions of line, conflicts of colours, or other details in a single instant. The work is static, and the eye's rhythm as it passes over the object of attention is chosen freely by the viewer and makes it possible to take in details and the whole simultaneously.

It is different with music, which proceeds over time, in an unceasing movement and modification of a variable nature and in a continuity that can even carry on when the music is silent, through rests and pauses. A melodic phrase, a development in sonority, a dynamic tension disappears and is followed by new impressions immediately afterwards. Thus, however intense a musical experience may be, it is only momentary and will remain ineffectual without some memory of what has passed. Without memory, no continuity can be created, and the details cannot be linked in a total impression, which is an important prerequisite for understanding music. Without memory, music will be like a fire that goes dead immediately after flaring up, without leaving a trace.

Memory first and foremost makes recognition possible. Since music has its existence in a given time span which the listener cannot influence, it is important that what has been previously heard be remembered and linked with what is heard now, so that what is heard later will be understandable and meaningful. In all music of any importance and quality, the different details have their necessary place within the whole. They must be perceived in their context and registered so securely that they do not escape attention. If they do, there will be gaps in the comprehension of the work, and it will soon become incomprehensible and, with that, tiresome. But if the details can be connected in the listener's consciousness, if they can be recognised as they recur later in a similar or maybe altered guise, they will be connected little by little in the listener's consciousness and will form the totality the nature and character of which thereby become comprehensible.

The music and its progress are given *a priori*, but listeners must themselves recreate the music in their minds to be able to grasp it, and for that to happen, the ability to recognise, to remember what is heard, is necessary. People who listen attentively and who have some experience in listening will easily be able to maintain their impressions and recreate them mentally, and thus have the opportunity to experience the music in the way it is intended by the composer and played by the performer.

This holds true not only for the first encounter with any particular work, but also when the music is heard again later. An earlier impression may certainly be changed later, perhaps be rejected and thereby lose its positive effect, but it may also be renewed, strengthened, and thus become of lasting value to the listener.

Whereas memory in itself is an unequivocal benefit, recognition may involve problems. Recognition may become a mental crutch if listeners remain satisfied with encountering the well-known. In that case they are not interested in new experiences, but rather may have a directly hostile attitude towards them, eventually bringing disarray into their musical universe and disturbance to the rational, considered standards which are the basis of their musical evaluations and aesthetic satisfaction. It is possible to find an undisturbed security and pleasure in the familiar merely because it is familiar, a passive satisfaction in listening to music that is devoid of unsettling surprises, and to have the quite simple desire not to permit disturbances to the easy comfort into which one expects to be lulled whenever what is already well known is heard once again. Nothing is allowed to be changed; everything must sound exactly as it is remembered; otherwise it will be rejected – which is tantamount to obstructing musical development and reducing and halting deeper understanding.

But recognition may also ease the way and open the door to new impressions, which may then produce an ever richer and broader understanding of the music. A renewed acquaintance with what is already known may uncover qualities previously missed, so that the music will be clearer in one's consciousness, will carry more meaning than was previously suspected.

Every substantial piece of music not merely bears repeating but requires it, so that it may unfold and be grasped in all its aspects by the listener; for it is given to very few people to comprehend a major musical work in its entirety on the first encounter with it.

Remembering music may thus bear a double sense, a passive or active effect long after the music is heard. Sometimes you catch yourself humming or whistling some little snippet or other of melody. There is nothing notable in that: it is common to hear people sing or whistle when they take a bath, clean up their room, weed the garden, go for a walk, or cycle down the street. This singing, humming or whistling may be a sign of serenity and good humour and may remain half-unconscious without being registered musically, regardless of whether it is self-created music or is something heard previously that spontaneously emerges at the time. This phenomenon has perhaps no deeper meaning, because it may remain a non-thinking humming the cause and effect of which never reach consciousness, either musically or existentially. But in many cases it involves quite conscious and concrete associations, tied to a remembered musical event. The memory of some definite event, a gathering, a chance encounter, a film or a play may bring a melody heard then out into consciousness, because it was closely linked with and deepened or characterised the event.

Conversely music, just like odours, can call forth events and bring them alive. For example, a theme from a Mozart piano concerto, when it is heard on the radio or at a concert performance, can give rise in many people to the image of Elvira Madigan and her fate, because they have seen a film in which the music was tied to the story.[7] Or a theme from Beethoven's *Appassionata* Sonata, which at one time could be heard everywhere, piercingly whistled by the bicycling delivery boys of the time, may in the same way have been the background in a film. The examples are legion, often originating in opera, theatre, and especially film: bits of melodies by Chopin, Tchaikovsky, Verdi and Schubert have all been on the street from time to time.

We cannot be sure whether the Madigan story or the films about composers are always remembered when fragments of Mozart or Beethoven melodies are whistled or hummed softly, but in all circumstances the melodies amount to symbols of a mood, of something that has made an impression. In such cases, any musical qualities there may play only a small role or none at all, because the music's function is secondary, and any bit of melody at all from an aria, a hymn or a song may become a symbol of a particular experience or mood.

While these associations rarely have any directly musical meaning, it is different with purely musical associations. There may be a melodic phrase the beauty, simplicity or expressiveness of which has acquired special meaning for someone, perhaps a fragment of a large-scale composition that emerges in the ear. And you can catch yourself having hummed or whistled it interminably, just as much to your satisfaction as to the obvious irritation of those around you.

Thus we must, when not alone, be resigned occasionally to allowing music to 'sing' only in the inner ear. For a composer, this is both normal and vital – perhaps a new work is about to break through the unconscious mists. But for the person who merely calls a work to mind because a pressing phrase has emerged in the ear, something nearly the same may occur. The association with the entirety of the work may be strong. Then it is not the events surrounding the work that are decisive for the memory, but the work itself, the qualities and the impression the music once made. Then the music is remembered spontaneously in its entirety through the little hummed phrase.

The direct and heard experience of a work is only brief in

---

[7] [The music in question is from the slow movement of the Piano Concerto No. 21 in C, ᴋ467.]

chronological time. But in the memory of the experience, and above all in the memory of the music itself, we are in possession of an asset as durable as it is valuable; the music stands brilliantly clear in our consciousness.

POSTLUDE

Quality and Substance

In the foregoing chapters, topics such as the composer's situation, the performer's problems, and the listener's possibilities in respect of music have been discussed. There, concepts such as 'quality' and 'substance' have often been mentioned, without making clear what they imply. I shall therefore try to approach these two concepts here, if only to provide some slight contribution to understanding the precariousness of linguistic formulations about what I must call musical reality.

When an interested person hears a piece of music, thinks it good, and in a discussion of it wants to make clear her or his point of view, it is generally natural to stress its *quality*. If asked what is really meant by that, the answer will often be an apparent justification: the music has substance, it has weighty content, it has meaning, and one feels it is good music. All this is airy talk because these shaky concepts are simply being shuffled around, and nothing much is being said other than that the music has made an impression for various reasons – which says more about a person's receptivity than about musical quality.

More practically, and without being misunderstood, we may speak of a work's *qualities*, and mean by that that the nature of its elements has 'good' properties. These properties can be evaluated, because the work's proportions, its material, technical and formal nature can be examined and described. If there is a balance among the parts and they are also in agreement with the familiar rules of the time, the conclusion can be positive, that the work has quality as a whole. Of course, the rules do change from time to time, so that a work from one period may lack those qualities which will be required in another period. Heard from a standpoint where style is fixed and rules obvious, a work written in a new manner will very often appear chaotic and anarchic, because it breaks with the familiar, and its own rules will not be grasped, since they are still unknown and are created only by and with the new work. On the other hand, a newly composed piece of music written on the basis of rules which are all too familiar and hackneyed will appear conventional, as imitation without interest or as a didactic exercise in an old style.

Under these conditions, which have obtained not least in the past century, no agreement can be reached on what the concept 'quality' actually covers. For some people, only what is well known may have quality; for others quality becomes synonymous with novelty. The concept will thus be relative, unusable as a norm for a fixed and unambiguous judgement of music.

But some difficulties may be overcome. With the historical insight which is attainable today, we can become capable of judging a work in relation to the time and the milieu in which it was written. To a certain extent we become familiar with its many-faceted background and may thus undertake a more objective and tenable evaluation.

To this extent the potential quality of a work could be established, had not the concept become value-laden so long ago. We can come close to an understanding of what is meant by quality only if the character and spiritual nature of the music are taken into consideration. Seen from an objective viewpoint, the concept has become charged with a metaphysical element, *substance*, which eludes unambiguous evaluation, although it is just this substance which, for many people, indeed for the vast majority, is the ultimate and crucial factor that must be considered in order to evaluate a musical work, regardless of its time and style.

Even if we are knowledgeable about contemporary styles and so can be in a position to evaluate the relationship between material, form and style in a work, it is not possible to judge substance objectively. Its indefinable metaphysics get in its way, because there is such close connection with emotional layers in the human mind that only a subjective statement has meaning. And of course limiting the apparent possibilities for broader agreement is our having to rely on 'I think...'.

I think, for example, that the *Radetzky* March of Johann Strauss Sr has quality, because there is a fine connection between the aims of the work, its technique, its musical substance, and its historical place. Mozart's G minor Symphony (No. 40, K550) is different (the main theme of its first movement having a striking similarity to the march theme in the Strauss). The thematic material and technique in the first movement are far more problematic in relation to the style of that time. It is not the bearer of a new style, nor does it have any immediate consequences for the further development of music. Nonetheless I must evaluate the Symphony as one of the greatest masterpieces ever written, against which the *Radetzky* March is for me merely well-disposed and attractive entertainment. The reason for my point of view must be an indefinable but also very secure feeling of a distinct difference in the spiritual natures of the two works.

The March strikes me as clear and precise, cheerful, straightforward and without particular problems: you know where you are with it, and understanding of the music is immediate.

Mozart's Symphony, on the other hand, is disquieting. I am not quite sure of what really happens in this music, whose light and accommodating surface seems banal on first analysis, and which first conceals and then gives me something completely indescribable, something beyond mood and state of mind, an inner knowledge about something which probably only a poet could reveal with words.

Seen in the light of the impression the Symphony gives, which is as strong as it is inexplicable, the technical and formal aspects seem masterly to me, without peer, and apparently wrought with disturbing ease, inseparable from the music's substance.

This evaluation does not contain a disguised hint that a larger composition has more quality than a smaller one, or that the simple and unproblematic work is of lesser value than the technically and psychologically more complicated one. Bach wrote intricate fugues which in all respects are of the highest quality – which can hardly be said of the many fugues which countless other composer-organists of his day worked out and which are just as complicated in their technique but are empty in their note-spinning.

On the other hand, Haydn has written masterpieces that are as accommodating as they are unsurpassed, works whose nature and technique are of a striking simplicity, while much of his contemporaries' music, similarly easily accessible, can be an empty, dismal, inconsequential wandering in the wilderness.[1]

As far as I can see, quality does not depend on the format

---

[1] [Further comments on Haydn may be found in the essay 'Haydn and Tradition', pp. 125–27.]

of the music or its complexity, nor on its particular gentleness or force of character – nor on whether it is what is called tasteful or tasteless. Neither the technical perfection alone nor the musical substance in itself is decisive for what I will call quality, but on the contrary: there must be a balance between the two. The musical substance, or content if you will, cannot be isolated from the musical material. The finest intentions are without value for the outside world if they are not manifested in tones, rhythms and sonorities in a way that is memorable and comprehensible. Without a close connection between the abstract, analysable material and the undefinable, indeed, inexplicable substance, the concept of quality will have no meaning.

But this still does not elucidate the problem sufficiently. Naturally, like many others, I have developed a sharper sense for musical quality, through experience and a deeper acquired knowledge over the course of time. And I can find quality as much in the simplest folk melody as in the most complicated piece of music. The result of this development is therefore sometimes that music which previously appealed to me instantly became less significant later on, perhaps because I then longed for the balance between intention and means upon which I had not insisted earlier. But it may also happen that I, like every other person, sooner or later become alienated from certain pieces of music, or at certain times become unreceptive towards specific musical impressions; that a musical work does not appeal any more to my intellect or my emotions, although I may still recognise its quality. And I know very well that it is not the music which has changed its substance or its significance, but that it is my own receptivity which – I hope only temporarily – has weakened. Usually I can hear with quite a lot of confidence whether a piece of music is substantial, whether it has quality, so it can be heard many times without losing its power, and thus become an inexhaustible source of musical experience. On each renewed acquaintance, a variety of possibilities can be uncovered layer by layer, at the same time as the work is recreated in one's consciousness as if it was being heard for the first time.

For example, a Haydn symphony may have a moment of surprise, an unexpected pause, a sudden drum stroke,[2] or an especially imaginative harmonic turn. It might be assumed that the surprise would weaken on repetition, but that is not the case.

The composer has taken us into an enchanted world, where every-thing that happens is just as wonderfully new on each repetition.

In these circumstances – and that basically means in any circumstance – no one can separate music's formal and techni-cal qualities from its substance. Thus we are able to express only a subjective attitude towards the substance and character of the individual work, and evaluate it on the basis of our own disposi-tion, predilection, knowledge and experience.

Since people themselves are such fluctuating receptors, and since the possibility that language can clarify the meaning of music is so uncertain, we must understand the concepts of quality and substance as *symbolic* expressions for the fact that a person, in a given piece of music and in a given situation, has ac-knowledged something that objectively satisfies the intellect and subjectively appeals to the emotions.

The Musical Experience

Besides the concepts of quality and substance, vague expressions like 'experience' and 'insight' have been mentioned here and there. They are all metaphysical in the sense that they lie out-side a human being's material and physical experience and cannot be precisely defined with words. My only prospect therefore is in circling around them, as I mentioned earlier, in the hope that I can shed light on these concepts in the musical context in this indirect way – and based on what I have learned myself.

As I have often stated, I have learned that music cannot produce any concrete statements which can be expressed in words, either about feelings or about events. I cannot label imi-tations of sounds from nature or the use of associations and sym-bols as concrete statements. I have also learned that, besides technical qualities, music can have a substance that can give me an experience that I cannot explain.

But since language is not capable of making concepts like sub-stance and the experiencing of music understandable, these con-

[2] [Holmboe refers here to Haydn's Symphony No. 94 in G. This work is popularly known in English as the 'Surprise' Symphony and in Danish and German as the Symphony 'With the drum stroke'. Both names refer to an unexpected dynamic accent near the beginning of the second movement which Haydn supposedly once said would wake up the somnolent members of the audience.]

cepts have often been disavowed, dismissed as sentimentality, romantic idealising, or self-delusion. People have maintained that music is organised sounds which can affect the human nervous system, that it is forms in motion, that only the notes themselves are the substance of music, and that all else is unreal fantasy.

It is true enough that music is organised sound which unfolds and takes shape in time. But that narrower definition, attractive and safe as it may be in theory, is in my experience insufficient. It still leaves room for recognition of artistic qualities, but it eliminates every possibility of the existence of a musical substance which can give people an experience.

I have undergone this inexplicable experience and cannot call it imaginary, for even if the substance of music and the musical experience cannot be analysed and evaluated, and with that be turned into words, these phenomena will be no less real.

A few of these experiences can perhaps shed light on what I mean. I cannot, for example, explain the effect Mozart's G minor Symphony has on me every time I hear it. The Symphony begins with an accompaniment, a broken G minor chord – and at once I am in another world with all my senses open to receive the music which I *know* is to come. I do not remember how it was the first time I heard the Symphony, but I am reasonably sure that I heard the beginning then only as 'a broken G minor chord'. It is not like that now. With that short introduction, the whole Symphony springs forth in a flash in my consciousness; the chord is like a portal on which everything that is to come is already engraved. It creates at once an intense expectation of the continuation to come and simultaneously, paradoxically enough, an assurance of encountering something unknown, something completely new every time I hear this music.

Something similar has often occurred with other music; for example, the famous drum-stroke in Haydn's G major Symphony is equally surprising every time I hear and take an intense interest in the music. Or Stravinsky's *Symphony of Psalms*: the first time I heard it, my professional interest did not manifest itself in a simultaneous conscious analysis of the musical events. The introductory chord on E caught me immediately, so that the music could continue to grow freely in my consciousness from this first sound into the complete work as a great and indescribable totality. This co-creative activity, together with feelings which arose spontaneously but which I could not account for, gave me an unforgettable musical experience, which was equally intellectual and emotional.

For me these experiences were reality, but whether it was the same reality as Mozart and Stravinsky may have had, I cannot know nor ever find out, even if I had an intense feeling that it could only be like mine.

Here I arrive at a problem which has given (and still gives) ample cause for exchange of opinion, and as much for one-sided and short-sighted attitudes. Many composers want naturally enough as direct a communication with their listeners as possible, to create contact by making clear their musical intention. This the composer can do, among other things, by literary means, programme notes or technical explanations, the use of symbols and associations or imitations in the music.

A chorale or funeral march introduced into a piece of music may symbolise a solemn mood and thereby characterise the music for the listener, just as a waltz may symbolise the pleasure of the dance, motion, and a show of life.

The premise is that the listener has the ability to make associations with something familiar, to connect the familiar with new impressions. Thus the conscious use of fragments from Classical or Romantic music in a contemporary collage-like style has, to be sure, a certain nostalgic, or perhaps ironic or satirical character, but it has meaning only if the quotations are known and recalled by the listener. Failing that, it simply either leads to bewilderment at the style or gives rise to a work that has the supreme ability to unite ostensibly incongruous components in a newly created whole.

An imitation of birds singing, mosquitoes dancing, or waves crashing may be recognised relatively easily, and misunderstood just as easily. The possibilities of more or less primitive associations are innumerable, and they may be exciting and amusing to follow, as in a guessing game. But this game, musically defensible as it may be, I can comprehend only as a surface phenomenon, an attempt to be amusing or interesting, to describe something which music is not capable of describing directly, and which is therefore 'unreal fantasy'.

In incidental music or in compositions with words, an ability in listeners to form images may be desirable and further the understanding of the artistic whole. But where music is only itself, where it is beyond every concrete conception, the conception and the image become a substitute, a non-musical element, whether the listener guesses 'right' or is on completely the wrong track. The conceptions a composer may have had when the music was being written are harmless only if they are not forced on the listener, and downright detrimental if it happens with means foreign to music.

Occasionally I have used quotations myself, a phrase from Gregorian chant, a folk melody, or a birdsong of four or five pitches as fused links in the artistic whole. I have undoubtedly also had non-musical ideas before I got down to writing a piece of music, but I have no clear recollection of this and thus cannot give concrete examples. These ideas must in any case have only been to get me going, because whether it was a matter of a particular mood, an image carried over from an event, or a more indefinite impression, what happened in every single case was that such ideas disappeared at the moment I began to work with notes. Whenever the music flowed forth and took shape, the notes and their particular problems were the only reality for me. And what is more, every non-musical idea which I might have had vanished completely whenever I later heard the music played. 'Only' the music itself was left, with its tensions, developments, and individual nature.

It is possible, and perhaps only human, that some composers cling to what was the 'impetus' for their piece of music, that in some way or other they try to relate the personal cause that set their mind in motion. But whatever gets the composer going by way of external events or experiences, by way of images or feelings, is, I must conclude, quite immaterial when the music is heard. They have no reality any more once everything is melted down in the ultimate material, the notes which cannot explain or say anything, but which nevertheless are capable of forging a direct connection with the mind, with human thought and feeling.

When I disregard in this way all non-musical associations and consider them as irrelevant, as inhibiting the real musical experience, it may, with some justification, be asked what remains after all.

The Ideal Listener

It has been said that what is heard depends on who is doing the hearing, and certainly that is a long-established truth. But it has particular relevance when, as here, it is a matter of the relationship of humanity to music and its potential for a direct musical experience of the music.

No one has exactly the same background for understanding music, and there are substantial differences in the way it is listened to. Some can find pearls where others only see sand, and the most gripping music may slip unnoticed past a closed mind.

However, there exist people who are able to listen in a way that I may call ideal. This kind of listening is not, whatever you might think, an unusual or even utopian phenomenon that is given only to the chosen few. With certain limitations and conditions, it is a potential which everybody has.

The most essential, indeed, the only really necessary thing is the positive and intuitive receptivity of the mind; but personal experience and a general musical background may to a large extent ease the way to a deeper understanding that makes possible the direct experiencing of music. On the other hand, a special technical knowledge, training and analytical capabilities are not absolute prerequisites.

The person who listens intuitively has well-developed receiving antennae which can rotate with lightning speed, sometimes turned towards the material of the work, its form and development, sometimes towards the emotional tensions and the inexplicable undercurrent which all vital music possesses. But these rotations are so quick that they bring about a continuous comprehension and coherent experience of the work. And the ideal listener must put into use all human capacities, emotional as well as intellectual, conscious as well as unconscious, so that the work may emerge and develop from beginning to end, so that it springs forth from the unconscious and takes shape for the listener as earlier it took shape for the composer.

The experience which such an intense listening can provide is, of course, not possible under all circumstances, but it nonetheless happens countless times to countless people. And every time, what the individual already knew is broadened, with respect not only to the individual work but to music altogether. Not only is the capacity for general human understanding developed, but one acquires the potential for reaching a direct insight which can be attained only with difficulty in other ways.

In their purest form, the joy and experiencing of music are direct and immediate. Music can be experienced as an expression of a consummate whole and can awaken a feeling of cosmic belonging. It can provide a mental jolt and in fortunate moments create an exaltation or lightening in the mind that takes the listener beyond everyday ego-consciousness. This is not a matter of flight from external realities, of passive oblivion, but a momentary state which activates the mind independently of chronological time, a state which can be felt as a direct opening for humanity into universal consciousness.

The person who listens to music in this way is certainly freed from the chaos in the composer's working methods – the often exceedingly vast amount of manual work, the doubt over the right choices, the struggle with material that may be stubborn – and this is not in the primary sense creative. But the listener's intense involvement in and understanding of the music open the way to a mental process of the same sort as the composer must have gone through previously. The ideal listener cannot be content with superficial emotional fluctuations or transformations into pictures and images, regardless of the fact that they may be felt to be pretty and useful impressions. It is crucial that a feeling arises of identity between the creating and receiving persons, when the listener experiences music as when it was created and thereby gains an insight, analogous to the composer's, into the musical and psychological sequence of events, into the relationship between part and whole, and into the dimension of time in which music unfolds.

Such a listener is therefore co-creative.

The Inexplicable in Music

Music has the potential to develop the creative, recreative, and co-creative capacities that reside in all of us. It can develop intellect as well as feeling, increase the individual's consciousness of self and surroundings. It is thus one of the fundamental conditions for an active and healthy cultural life.

But little as the phenomenon of culture is a fixed and immutable asset, an insured property, so it is with creative abilities. They must be renewed, kept alive and developed through ever new challenges. If that does not happen, these abilities will wither away, make humanity poor and rootless, transform the mind in a negative direction, and thereby open the way to destructive thinking and conduct.

Music is a disguised energy source which has a clear and strong influence on thought and mind, an immediate effect which can reach far beyond the merely entertaining. Much is written about music, but when I consider the subject, as here, in a more psychological perspective, I must recognise the paradoxical in the relationship between the descriptive word and the inexplicable in music.

On the one hand, we can claim that music is exclusively forms moved in sound, that it cannot have any other substance, and that its assertions are as abstract as those of mathematics. On the other hand, it is precisely the substance that can be meaningful, be concretely present, produce a strong emotional impact and thought-provoking impulses. Music cannot say anything, yet it says so much. It is readily accessible to everyone, but nevertheless difficult to grasp. It is not logical, but can have a strict logic in its elaboration.

Such paradoxes are, of course, only apparent. They are pseudo-opposites which arise from verbal formulations and visual ideas which can say nothing about the nature of music itself. It may thus seem absurd to wish to write about those aspects of music which words must relinquish. However, I believe that we must point out again and again the many particular relations there are between humanity and music, and that we discuss the subject in a perspective different from the purely technical, regardless that we can never get to the bottom of, but must constantly circle around, the inexplicable.

That is what I have tried to do here.

OTHER ESSAYS

EPILOGUE
from the book *Interlude*

All music must necessarily depend on sound, and all sounds may become music. But the tone is superior to other sounds, because it is not bound to things. It is born of matter and carries information about it, but it frees itself and undulates as an incorporeal vibration out in space.

The tone is both concrete and abstract – not as firmly tied to things as the rhythmical noise of a machine, the banging of a piano lid, or the screech from a car that brakes abruptly, nor as purified of every earthly thing as the cool sound of an electronic oscillator.

The tone is transformed sound. It has become a quality which alone among all sounds embraces simultaneously the heftily earthbound and the unencumbered ethereal. We cannot free ourselves entirely from the power of the tone over our minds, no matter how much we might wish to cultivate everyday concrete noises or electronic sound abstractions, because the tone is both of body and of spirit and thus contains all those unsuspected possibilities which, together with its sisters, it gives to people in the art of music.

But the tone has existence only in the dimension of time. It has a duration and is thus from the outset connected with rhythm through its varying length and changing accents. From the simplest folk melody to the most complicated piece of music, it is the relationship between the two, tone and rhythm, that creates the laws of music.

And of all laws, the fundamental law of *tension* is the first and last, that from which all changing rules and conventions derive, that which connects humanity and music from the first instant a tone or a rhythm is perceived. It is the tension between the tones, rhythms and harmonies that holds them together in a changing equilibrium and turns them into music. The simplest melodic line, the simplest rhythm, and the most primitive harmony create tension – and if this fails, the coherence and meaning of music also disappear.

Tension implies that there is a resistance to be overcome, that with all musical energy there is a constraint, just as the stone which is thrown up into the air is constrained in its motion by the attraction of the earth.

Tension results when a melodic line rises, when the rise is felt as an ever-increasing expenditure of energy and an attempt to escape from the law of gravity that applies to music. But every melodic curve has a climax which cannot be overstepped without the continuity snapping. If that happens, the melody will burst into ornamental particles and cease to be melody.

Tension comes about when dynamic, sonorous or rhythmic energies intensify; when, in the attempt to escape the moderate degree of strength, the restful harmony and the regular pulsation, they approach the limit which they too cannot overstep without the connection bursting and the tension ceasing.

Every musical development creates tension. It has its inherent limits, varying according to the nature, bearing and format of the individual work, but perceivable as tension only if it can be heard and understood, either in relation to an equilibrium or inertia in the material, or in relation to other forces which tend in the opposite direction. This means that the more composers wish to increase the tension, the more they must promote the forces that maintain the equilibrium.

If we wish to speak at all of music as communication, as art and *œuvre*, music must necessarily be a continuity and a whole; and its multifarious forces, operating in all directions, must be co-ordinated and balanced. The stronger are the composers' outbursts of emotion, the more they must bring in will and command in order to curb the unconstrained demands of the emotions – inside themselves they must find that place where emotion and intellect are united, where chaos is transformed into cosmos.

For humanity, Apollo and Dionysus stand as two essentially different principles, like the masculine and the feminine, form and content, choice and chance, the abstract and the concrete. Separately they are barren; in conflict with each other they are destructive; but when they work together and become one, life results. This life is reflected in the music, in its infinity of nuances between rest and motion, and in its tensions between growth and control.

When music is true, it constantly transforms chaos into cosmos in an unbroken process, a chain reaction which lasts as long as the music is heard. And the converse: when music constantly transforms chaos into cosmos, then it is true.

With this, the meaning and logic of words cease. Thought goes in circles and must recognise its own limitations, for just as it is impossible for a child to capture the sun's rays with its hands, so it is impossible to grasp and explain with words music's innermost essence.

Only music itself can grasp and explain music.

ON THE EXPERIENCING OF TIME
from the book *Interlude*

The basic material of music, sound, has its existence in time, and we must necessarily regard the relationship of tones to one another as motion in time and space, as duration and shape. Sound waves reach our ears successively but are combined by our consciousness and become a shape. We know at once whether an individual tone is short or long, weak or strong, passive or dynamic; and through these and many other qualities, we learn not only the individuality of the tone but also the nature and structure of the shape. Gradually, as a musical work proceeds, it is established in our consciousness and will exist ultimately as a whole. Without the ability to understand music as form, to remember details and grasp connections, music will be to us a meaningless succession of isolated episodes, just as a person's limbs and organs are meaningless by themselves and only as parts of a whole (the person) acquire context and purpose.

Whereas we may consider musical form as the realisation of the material in time, what we call musical material or matter is a more abstract and theoretical concept. The tone, its constitution in the horizontal and vertical directions (whence melody and harmony), is normally called 'material'. We can take parts out of context, we can count measures and series, isolate a chord or a motive, which we are subsequently in a position to analyse and evaluate. We can obtain information that assists us in our efforts to understand what happens in the music when we hear it later; but we cannot, even through a really brilliant analysis, find out what musical experience is or learn to undergo it.

The situation is reversed when music is being heard, when it is being experienced in time and context, whether it takes place in our inner or our outer ears. If we try to analyse details or courses of events while the music is sounding, such attempts will invariably influence or interrupt the course of events and so also our experience of the music in the dimension of time.

Now it is both very easy and very hard to discuss the concept of time. We have measurements that are just as firm for time as they are for weight, length, area and volume. These measurements can be expressed precisely and incontestably in minutes, grams and metres, a useful fact of which we endlessly avail ourselves every day. On the other hand, we also learn daily that measurements alone cannot tell us whether an object is long or short, heavy or light, big or little, because these are relative, dependent on the surroundings, the function of the object, and the impressions we have of these things. The ten minutes we spend in a dentist's waiting–room give us quite a different sensation of length of time than the ten minutes during which we are having an interesting conversation. We think that a piece of music that bores us lasts much longer than a piece of the same length that captivates us.

Psychology and past experience can tell us that especially intense or beautiful sections of a musical work usually go by in shortened time, while sections that lack interesting details or which create a tension, an expectation of something to come, are perceived in lengthened time. (This is surely one of the reasons that performing musicians often feel the need to have a crescendo accompanied by an accelerando, and so eliminate the psychological lengthening of time.)

With a stopwatch we may measure the length of a musical work, whereas the time-experience we get through it may not be measured and may be described only in general terms. The mechanical ticking of the watch is superseded in music by the live and varied pulsations of rhythm. The regular passing of minutes and hours is replaced by the irregular but controlled lengthenings and shortenings that make time alive for us. We experience special and varied time durations that free us from the everyday, more mechanical awareness of time, and which make it clear to us that when it is a question of musical experience, only the time-duration created by the music comes into consideration. Physical time ends up as a fiction.

Now it can be rightly said that the experience of time in the waiting-room, just as during the conversation, is also special in relation to the time of the watch, and that countless similar examples can be mentioned which can easily be experienced. The psychological laws are, of course, valid to the same degree, regardless of whether the cause is a swollen finger, a brilliant conversation or a Haydn symphony. But apart from the different aesthetic and emotional impressions we receive from, respectively, the finger, the conversation, and the symphony, the art of music can present us with a far richer and more differentiated experience of time than any other medium we know.

Music has ordinarily unprecedented possibilities for shading and varying our sensation of time, to make it both free and controlled, to have us undergo a succession of time events that is independent of external associations, images and thoughts, and which is probably the fundamental condition for the musical experience. On the other hand, our capability of experiencing those immeasurably varied time differentiations is, of course, dependent on our own capacity to adapt, to free ourselves from ourselves and our mechanical sensation of time, to enter receptively into that dimension of time which music creates in us.

Just as we acquire elementary space-experience through harmony, we acquire elementary time-experience through rhythm. Rhythm is at once a contrast to and the prerequisite for the formal elements: motive, phrase, section and movement, which in turn produce the large rhythms of music, its structure and form.

With these concepts we try to maintain an awareness of law and order in music, knowing well that chaos lies just underneath this order, since all the elements of music endlessly undergo little alterations. Rhythm is not a mechanical cutting up of time, and in no piece of music are there two measures of precisely the same dimensions, so that the same motive or theme can never recur in precisely the same way. And just as the placing of a motive in a tension-creating or a tension-relaxing passage gives two different temporal sensations of the motive, conscious shifts in tempo affect not only the dimensions of the individual elements but also their individuality and character. Even slight shifts can alter the nature of a musical work, and one motive played in two quite different tempos can be transformed into two motives, each with its own individuality.

This constant embracing of a living and freely flowing rhythm with forces that are included to control and shape it is experienced immediately. But every attempt to reflect and evaluate *while the music is playing* is doomed to failure, for we cannot possibly manage to hold on to a detail before it is gone and a new one has turned up, and if we are capable of holding on to it, we must let the music flow right past us. Musical analysis must, therefore, metaphorically speaking, stop time in order to get the music out of its temporal existence and into a spatial form that can be analysed. With that the experience-possibility is dropped, and thus we cannot simultaneously analyse and experience music.

This well-known relation has been regarded as a dualism, and furthermore, the concept has been transferred to the relation between content and form or, stated more objectively, between the shaping forces and the completed form-pattern. Here, however, it is overlooked that the form-patterns are to the form-possibilities as a pot is to clay, as a match flame is to fire, as the concrete object is to the abstract concept; it is overlooked that form arises from the possibilities of the material, makes them concrete and produces the patterns.

Nor is it to be presumed that the relation between analysis and experience – concepts which at once complement and exclude each other – can be called dualistic in the usual sense of the word.

Here there is a similarity to the situation in atomic science, when it is a question of results achieved under different experimental conditions. These, writes Niels Bohr,[1] cannot be combined in one single picture, but must be considered as complementary in the sense that only together do the phenomena exhaust the contingent data on the objects. Both Bohr and other atomic physicists suggest points of similarity with complementary relations within other domains of human cognition, thus, for example, between thought and feeling or between instinct and reason. In a series of lectures, the atomic physicist Werner Heisenberg[2] uses the same expression and also mentions the musical situation:

> We maintain that the situation of complementarity is not at all limited to the world of the atom. We come upon it perhaps when we reflect on a decision and on the motives for our decision, or perhaps when we have the choice between the enjoyment of music and the analysis of its structure.

[1] [Danish atomic physicist (1885–1962).]

[2] [German (1901–76); the quotation comes from 'Language and Reality in Modern Physics', Chapter 10 of *Physics and Philosophy* (English translation published by Allen and Unwin, London, 1959).]

It seems as if the recognition of the complementary in our situation uncovers several points in common, not only between natural science and music but indeed between art and science. In every direction, one looks today for unity behind diversity, one tries to find the laws in common for micro-and macrocosmos, to perceive humanity from a comprehensive view and to arrive at comprehensive forms in art. We must go all the way back to the Renaissance to find a situation that matches ours and for which re-evaluation is important to the same degree.

Just as in our time we are gaining understanding of time as dimension, with all the consequences in thought and feeling that will follow from that, in the Renaissance they arrived at space as dimension. Then as now, humanity was standing at the forefront of a new perception of itself and its environment, which was given meaning not only in astronomy and other natural sciences, but also in art. Thus, there is hardly any doubt that the pursuit of perspective in painting and harmony in music was a direct result of the new perception of space.

Furthermore, it is quite clear that the development of music did not take place later without dependence on or connection to the attitude of the surrounding culture. The same thoughts, feelings and ideas seem to arise in several places at once, they wash in like waves over the whole domain of culture, produce eddies with opposing currents, and are recognised afterwards, when the water has calmed down, as a pattern of culture. The mere contemporary, who finds himself in the middle of the eddies and the suction, may have difficulty in recognising his own situation.

STRAVINSKY'S
SYMPHONY OF PSALMS

It is possible that the gramophone and radio are dangerous new technological advances, because they seduce us so easily into purely passive enjoyment of music; and it is certain that the gramophone can never replace the concert hall with its acoustical conditions and direct contact. But how would we have become familiar with many of music's masterworks if we had not had the gramophone? And it acquires a quite special significance when it comes to new music, with its frequently substantial orchestral and technical demands.

Thus it is fortunate that, for example, most of Stravinsky's major orchestral and chamber-music works are recorded on disc; otherwise we would have had no chance, or at most only one, to hear them.

In spite of defects in sound and unpleasant aesthetic qualities, it is possible through the gramophone to get a strong impression of a musical work. Indeed, one remembers what an experience it was, what a shock was felt, when a work like the *Symphony of Psalms* was first heard in one's own room. Every sound, every note in the work is familiar now; nonetheless, one needs only to put the stylus on the record once more, whenever one desires to hear the work, and it emerges again with the same freshness and power as on the first occasion. One listens with the same wonder and with an ever-increasing understanding.

When what is called our technological century can, among other things, make important musical works generally available, that alone must make up for any urge to go back to the 'cosiness' of an earlier period merely on grounds that technology is *dangerous*. It is correct that in the sense of machinery, a technology is dangerous, just as in an artistic sense it is tedious, when it is an *end* in itself. But that is precisely why it is the task of our time to seek to master what technology there *is*, and thereby make it a legitimate, even necessary *means*, rather than give it a wide berth and act as if it does not exist. Only then does the situation become really dangerous.

It is very difficult to accuse Stravinsky of technical deficiency. On the contrary, his unique skill in this regard is always stressed, and he is sometimes accused a bit acidulously of having an alleged lack of warmth, soul, poetry, etc. If these very critics knew that precisely the same was said of many of the great composers of the past, they might treat these notions a little more carefully. As far as Stravinsky's *Symphony of Psalms* is concerned, such criticism lapses. It is a brilliant achievement of the composer's creative genius, a rare example of synthesis of compositional will and vigour with technical command. The work is classical insofar as it is consummate in its artistic balance and supreme command of the materials; every note, every dynamic nuance, every instrumental detail is an expression of Stravinsky's genius. The conflict, the tension in the work does not lie, therefore, in the composer's struggle with material and form – which is, tragically, what we may often hear in symphonic music of the Romantics, where the concept *form* may be a problem which, as it were, lies outside the music and is thus insoluble.

As soon as one of the elements of a piece of music or one of its causes is singled out and treated independently of the others, there appears a flaw, often fatal, in the finished work of art. By 'elements' I mean here not only melody, harmony and rhythm, but also form and even (potentially) instrumentation; and by 'cause' I mean, for example, working calm, high spirits, inspiration and the collective emotion. All these factors must work together, and the more they are in balance, the stronger the work of art will be.

For contemporary composers it is natural that music *cannot describe* emotion and its nature, or in other words: emotion is *not the goal*. It may actually be said that emotion is the *driving force*, the *cause* that gets composers to express themselves in what is for them the natural medium: music. This emotional cause – no matter what kind – may be immaterial to listeners when they are confronted with the work of art. The work must be able to stand alone, without explanation or justification, as a synthesis of emotional tension, compositional power and technical command.

The tremendous tension of the *Symphony of Psalms* is due to

Tivoli, Copenhagen, 1959: Holmboe listens as Stravinsky walks past a photograph of Nielsen (photograph by Meta May Holmboe)

something purely emotional, an ethical-religious conflict. But the music does not illustrate the emotional development that is sensed in the text; in the symphony there is no goal, no propensity beyond a purely musical one. Even if Stravinsky had not said so in as many words, it would still be clear that his purpose in the *Symphony of Psalms* has been the simple one of realising a *musical work* which as much as possible satisfies his intentions.

The text to the three-part choral symphony, fragments of three psalms from the Old Testament, was put together by Stravinsky himself. It is sung in Latin by a four-part mixed chorus where women's voices are replaced by boys' voices. This is in itself quite unusual, but there are other peculiarities in the score. The clarinets, which have so often been Stravinsky's favourite instruments, are lacking; violins and violas are similarly missing.

In return, two pianos and a harp play a prominent role, partly by their rhythmic emphasis, partly by the sonorities they produce.

It is important to realise that these external instrumental conditions are not random but that on the contrary they are witness to Stravinsky's having made sure that the apparatus he is dealing with produces the best possible expression for his musical will; and at the same time they disclose the nature of this will. Boys' voices are clearer, cooler and less subjectively expressive than women's voices, and the instruments that lend themselves to burlesque figuration and inflated melody are removed. Stravinsky wants to have an obediently 'objective' orchestral medium which cannot vulgarise his musical intentions, but which will be just the right means of expression for the power and the clear lines of his melodies, the severity of his rhythm and the incredible richness and variety of his sonorities.

Anyone who examines Stravinsky's output must be astonished at how comprehensive a genius he is. He can accommodate the most marked contrasts without ever making the wholeness and balance of the work of art suffer. These contrasts, admittedly, are as a rule of a purely external kind: if you go beneath the surface in his works, you find them kindled by the same fire.

Among Stravinsky's works we find two both of which are influenced to a marked degree by religion, and both of which are monumental works that stand out, not merely in contemporary music but in European music altogether. One work is the *Symphony of Psalms* and the other is *The Rite of Spring*, which was written nearly twenty years earlier. In a curious way these two works complement each other.

The Rite, the great ballet, is based on movement, stylised dance – on extremely complicated rhythms and harsh sounds. The religiousness which underlies it is nature-influenced, ecstatic and primitive, which the relationship between people and nature-god can be. The *Symphony* is based on the chorus, the human voice, which has a mollifying effect on the overall sound. The tension is hardly less than in *The Rite*, only in the *Symphony* it is under a supreme control which has no equal. The religiousness behind the *Symphony* is of a more ethical kind; there can be no doubt that it is the relationship found in the Psalms between humanity and God that must have brought Stravinsky to write this work.

But it is the same man who wrote both the *Symphony of Psalms* and *The Rite*; behind both works we find the same austere, often coolly distant attitude which is so remarkably opposed to the almost passionate striving that is evident everywhere...

The *Symphony of Psalms* was written for the Boston Symphony Orchestra. It was completed in August 1930 and first performed simultaneously by Koussevitzky in Boston and Ansermet in Brussels in December 1930. It has since been performed all over Europe. In Copenhagen it was performed in 1934 under the direction of Anders Rachlew; but there was no more than the one performance. It is now nearly 10 years later, and so if we had not had the gramophone...!

IN MEMORY OF
CARL NIELSEN

The sublime in art defies definition and is beyond the grasp of most people. Even the most meticulous study of an artist's personality offers no clue to what this thing is any more than does the most painstaking analysis of his works.

The contemporary public, although one would think that it had every chance of a direct appreciation of the artist and the conditions under which he works, is nearly always at a loss and divides itself into two separate camps: one whose objection to anything modern and prejudice against the unfamiliar will prompt the other to rave in fatuous idolatry.

And posterity, offered the possibility of a truer and more unbiased appreciation of the masterpiece, appears to be too far removed from the artist. The human element behind the masterpiece has become an abstraction, a mere biographical item, and so any spontaneous realisation of the affinity between the man and his work is not possible any more.

Carl Nielsen shared the fate of almost all other eminent composers. While young he was in the eyes of his contemporaries a radical and a rebel, a scorner of convention and a scoffer at beauty. Later, however, he was to attain a pre-eminence that overshadowed everything else. He became the centre of a magnetic field, evoking the anger and jealousy of many a lesser magnet. And now, a hundred years after his birth, his name has become a household word. He is a composer whose works are played, yet has not the power to stir the minds of the young of today. Or has he?

Around the centenary of his birth so much will be written and related about this man and his works. New details and fresh appreciations will abound, for, after all, a man's work is never a finished and complete thing. It will go on changing forever before the eyes of each new generation.

As for myself, I belong to a generation that was too young to receive more than a fleeting impression of Carl Nielsen the man. In fact, I met him only once, but then that meeting became the turning point of my future and career.

My approach to Carl Nielsen's music changed in the course of time in a manner that, whilst it may not be said to be typical, is sure to present certain familiar features. While very young I was uninterested in his music, or perhaps it was rather aversion that I felt. What music of his I knew, and I am afraid that it was not a great deal, I found to be either repellent to me or suggestive of a simplicity bordering on the trite. In due course all this changed and I was to meet his music, in particular the symphonies, with an open mind, each fresh confrontation adding to my admiration.

At the time I sucked in nourishment uncritically where I could find it, and Carl Nielsen certainly had plenty of sustenance to offer, no matter whether he expressed himself in words or music. Later, following other paths and acquiring a more critical and discerning mind, I was to view Carl Nielsen's music in a wider perspective, one that included such names as Sibelius and Bartók. The years have passed, and today, a hundred years after his birth, Carl Nielsen's work is to me a monument, and I feel that like any true monument it will keep alive the memory of both himself and his day.

I think that one may safely say that great composers show but a transient and rather perfunctory interest in the invention of new mediums. If they employ a particular idiom or device, it is because it urges itself as a fit vehicle for their ideas, but the means is to them never the end, and if they happen to devise some novel means of expression, it is as often as not the result of endeavours directed towards quite different matters.

Of course, Carl Nielsen made use of the musical resources that had currency in his day. But he did not fritter away his genius in futile pursuit of technical subtleties or studied individuality. The distinctiveness of his idiom was the result of his will to expression and creative powers. The means which he employed acquired life and force, became expressions of his individuality and brought deliverance solely because they derived their life and force from his creative genius.

This explains why his work has survived and will live on. Very likely it has little appeal to the young of today as a source of inspiration, for it does not indicate any new departure in technique, nor does it suggest any specific artistic trend. Its importance lies in the fact that to the young of every new age or generation it will bear evidence of a powerful mind prevailing over the material and refusing to be led astray, that it is a manifestation of spiritual force, a life-work rising above mere ephemeral trends, and for that reason classical.

HAYDN AND TRADITION

I think it is a common assumption that many young composers equate tradition and stagnation; and that is certainly in keeping with youth's traditional clash with the idols of the older generation or its struggle against derivatively empty phrases and forms, which a creative composer must feel are stale and lifeless and therefore loudly repudiates.

Young composers naturally are right to fight what they feel is burdensome tradition, a dead weight, which they must discard in their independent and free striving after new content and new forms. But they are not right in summarily equating tradition, stagnation and imitation. The consequences of that attitude may be catastrophic for those same young people; and if they cling to it past a normal rebellious phase, they will merely achieve a pseudo-liberation which all too easily ends up in rootless sterility.

Tradition is often regarded as a constraint and (especially after the First World War) has been likened to stagnation. This is undoubtedly due to the multiple meanings of the word. The concept is not a fixed one; for it may certainly involve simple imitation, derivativeness which is perhaps correct but insipid, but it may also mean a foundation of experience, which for the composer may be a standard and an inspiring stimulus to fresh creative work with the conditions of a new age. I must understand the concept in this latter sense, and as far as I can recall, as a composer I have always regarded tradition as a cultural heritage which was felt not to be an enforced obligation but a merciful gift.

When I was quite young, I was interviewed by a journalist who in the course of the conversation asked which composers I was especially influenced by: the interviewer obviously expected that I would repudiate the classical tradition and mention exclusively the great contemporary musical vanguard.

When I mentioned Haydn first of all, the journalist was both surprised and dismayed, because my answer was not at all in agreement with the traditional picture, the one he too had formed of youth; and that a young modern composer could be influenced by an antique like Haydn was in his eyes something close to unnatural.

In the interview there was no room for a closer justification, but here it is, many years later.

That admiration for Haydn's music is instinctive, that it is anchored in an immediate attraction without any reflection is, to be sure, a principal cause; but it is hardly a sufficient explanation, the less so as several composers might be mentioned for whom I have an absolute and deep admiration, but who do not have this special attraction. On the other hand, an attempt to give an adequate impression of Haydn's greatness as a composer is not possible here, so I must be content to point out a few features which may perhaps shed a little light on the matter.

On a superficial hearing, Haydn's music is uncomplicated, accommodating and easily accessible. Its humour, its drama and its unerring formulation of concise material are understood just as readily as a fairy-tale is understood by any child. Many people stop there in their evaluation of Haydn, resign themselves to it, and in so doing spread around the notion of 'Papa Haydn', the good and kind composer who writes very nice music, easy to listen to, but without the depths of a Mozart or a Beethoven. But we must not be fooled: Haydn's music is like the fairy-tale, or like an iceberg. Under the visible (or audible) surface unsuspected powers are hidden which are released and comprehended only by a receptive, reflective and sensitive mind. It would take far too much space to go further into this, to become immersed in his symphonies, quartets and sonatas and describe the fantastic, effortless balance between form and content that is so assured that you do not think about it for a minute when you listen to the music. Haydn's form is created directly by the spontaneous, richly varied content and is thus unique for every single work.

There is, however, one item which from my point of view is important to bring out, namely, Haydn's close connection with folk music. This is due not so much to a direct adoption of tunes from the folk music by which he was surrounded, and knew so well – attractive songs and dances of Austrian, Hungarian, Croatian, Slovakian origin – but in far deeper measure to the fact that his music has its roots in folk music. No matter how complicated, subtle and refined his form and technique may become over the years, he always preserves the spontaneously human and straightforwardly musical utterance, which is fundamental to all folk music.

Many composers, and perhaps basically all the great ones, have their roots deep down in the primal layers of the human mind, from which all folk music arises; and they all have the ability to join the simple, the clear and the possibly naive to a fairly advanced technique and intellectual mode of expression. The overall power of *individual renewal* and *collective tradition* has always been important in European music. Without renewal, music turns into a weak echo, a banality; but if tradition is cut away, music will be dehumanised. It will turn into cerebral concoctions and empty postulation.

Technique, style and mode of expression have changed, both before and after Haydn, in accord with the changing times. But Haydn was innovative to an unusual extent and developed his highly personal and intellectually sophisticated music in the light of a powerful tradition. Thus he can be an example to any era, but like the other great composers from the past and the present, he cannot be imitated without fatal consequences. For mere imitation will simply betray tradition, which is a gift and a stimulus to renewal.

A LITTLE STRING TRIO

One doesn't right away remember very much about one's first appearance before the public. Maybe because a debut is rarely as definitive and significant an affair for a creative artist as for a performer, and this in turn resulting from it being chance – not competence – that most often controls when a composer first gets to try a composition on the public. Rarely is much made of the matter. Of course, there are exceptions; for just as painters can make their debut with a whole exhibition, it does happen that composers make theirs with a whole concert, and then the appraisers can duly bring out their tape measures and slide rules.

Well, my case was not one of the exceptions: in November 1932[1] a little string trio was performed along with some other new Danish chamber music. That was my debut, and it came off calmly and was largely ignored, but it ended with Danish sandwiches, red wine and coffee after the concert (there was also beer, but I don't drink beer) and a short comment in the paper the day after. This, my first encounter with the papers, was not exactly encouraging. We composers-to-be got to hear various truths that were not delicately worded. One of us learned that he should have a spanking for wasting his valuable time on anything like composing. Nor was there anything spied in another (that was me) that made much of an impression. There may well have been talent, but there was no real energy noticeable behind all the solemnity. The young composers had no feeling at all and the whole thing amounted to form and notes that merely glittered in themselves.

Here I cannot help straying a bit from the subject, for later I met up with far more amusing and lively examples of a

---

[1] [2 November, to be exact. The trio is listed as No. 'b', M. 43 in the catalogue of Holmboe's works. It precedes his 'official' Op. 1 by some four years and 36 compositions. Its first performers were Gerhard Rafn (violin), Niels Borre (viola) and Torben Anton Svendsen (cello); Borre (1897–1960) was a violinist and violist in the Danish Radio Orchestra and a member of several Danish string quartets.]

reviewer's honest indignation being recast into caustic and fanciful wit. Only a decade after my debut, my *Notturno* for woodwind received the following tirade in Sweden, printed on *Aftonposten*'s pink paper: 'His music demonstrated impotence pure and simple. Can you imagine a middle-aged man snoring at noon? It's not really hard, but why describe it in music?'

That man I would like to have met, but the war kept me from getting to Sweden at the time the concert took place. So I had to be content with having his epic framed and merrily quoting it afterwards. In addition, a decade later a Danish critic was, if anything, just as thoroughly outraged over my *Suono da Bardo* for piano. First the reviewer lays it on thick and describes it as 'both long and boring, in places even clumsy and affected in its primitivism', but he puts it on a still higher plane in finding extreme terms for his rich graphic fantasy: 'one imagined a stark naked savage on the main street in rush hour'. Him I would also like to have met. And every time I walk down the main street in Aarhus, I hope to meet the savage – but so far in vain.

But now back to the debut work. I am ashamed to admit that I can't remember it, and I won't look for the music to refresh my memory – that wouldn't be fair play. By contrast, I can remember quite a lot of my colleagues' music. There was a string quartet by Syberg[2] which I found was a splendid and skillful piece of work, and there was a violin sonata by Foerlev[3] which I still have a pretty clear impression of; in addition there were some songs by Schierbeck[4] and finally a quartet by Langgaard[5] that I didn't really like. On further consideration, there is nothing very odd in not being able to remember one's own little trio of 1931. I am one of those who try to forget what they've written as fast as possible after they've finished it in order to make room for new works. It's always been like that, and it still is.

[2] [The only string quartet by Franz Syberg (1904–55), organist and composer, who stopped composing in the early 1940s.]

[3] [Aage Foerlev (1911–1986), known mainly as a pianist and teacher.]

[4] [Poul Schierbeck (1888–1949), best known for his vocal music.]

[5] [The Third String Quartet by Rued Langgaard (1893–1952), organist, composer and conductor. His expressionism rooted in late Romanticism (which never has appealed to Holmboe) lay outside the main trends in Danish music in the first half of the twentieth century. In Denmark recently there has been much more interest in Langgaard's music than before.]

Of course, a composer can't forget what he has written just like that; but he may let it disappear, let it sink from consciousness to the unconscious, where it is put in storage. Anyhow, he may assume that happens, since he does after all make progress in one way or another. Furthermore, I have noticed that compositions with which the composer himself was dissatisfied and which he therefore tried especially quickly to forget and pack away, show up later – often much later – in a new and more successful guise. Naturally it has turned into a quite different work, and there need not be the slightest resemblance between the two compositions; but after it's all over, the composer knows rather precisely that what was problematic in the first piece is solved in the second by itself, as it were, without the intervention of the intellect.

As I said, a composer's debut may occur somewhat accidentally, but it is hardly accidental *that* it occurs. One certainly doesn't simply go and write a trio (it takes *some* preparation), and still less does one without further ado get the chance to have it performed. And there is indeed a long and unpleasant story behind this trio, a time full of sweat and tears, of financial difficulties, of despondent spells and unsuccessful compositions, but also a time of successfully creative periods and a few semi-private performances.

Much better than the trio I remember a string quartet,[6] for example, which was performed at a matinee at the Conservatory, where I was a student, in 1929. I remember it so well because it was the very first work of mine that got played, and because I wrote it all bit by bit under the guidance of my teacher Finn Høffding.[7] Admittedly, the quartet doesn't amount to much, but it meant a lot to me that I managed to hear it, and I still regard it with a certain affection, for without the work on it I certainly would hardly have been able later to tackle the writing of string quartets.

In the following year I got a few little things played at art exhibitions; these were not significant items, and they are accordingly put aside and forgotten today, but the trio was the first work that was performed at a genuine concert with critics and all that –

[6] [Probably the String Quartet in D minor, M. 17, which precedes Holmboe's 'official' String Quartet No.1 by seven string quartets and 19 years.]

[7] [Høffding (b. 1899) is well known as a composer, teacher, administrator and author.]

thus I must call it the debut-work, and that's why there was a certain real nervous tension at its performance.

It would be wrong to say that there was sheer joy over the criticism. All hopes were intact when the newspapers were opened the morning after the concert, but they burst like soap-bubbles, and an ice-cold shower was the result. Those showers are said to be healthy, and maybe that one was, but anyhow a shock was felt the effects of which lingered a long time. Until the debut, there was very little self-confidence – a swinging like a pendulum between a feeling of absolute incompetence and a pretty clear idea that something both could and would be achieved; not so little after all. And now it seemed that the critics were upsetting the apple-cart, and the thought arose that there definitely wouldn't be many composers around if the critics got their way and weeded out all the growing shoots when they couldn't even tell the wheat from the chaff.

But that's not really the way things go, and in my case the shock hardened, so I decided then and there on my second alternative: that there was something to be achieved and that it would be achieved; and so one is always helping to see to it that the critics get their daily bread. Incidentally, one has learned since to understand the particular difficulties and problems of criticism, and to distinguish between the reviewers worth reading and the ignoramuses, between those who understand their many-sided responsibilities and the others.

Back then, though, the criticism was neither helpful nor encouraging to a young composer. The help came from another quarter – namely at the sandwich table after the concert, where the composers and performers gathered and discussed the evening's achievements. This festive postlude, which really was something, took place at the home of Aksel Agerby (then President of the Association of Young Musicians),[8] who was just as sociable and sporting as he was dogged and stubborn when necessary. There were many of us, and we took up a lot of space in the small rooms on Larslejstræde. I remember that the painter Fritz Syberg had come over from Funen to hear his son's quartet, and a good number of those musicians who today are leaving

---

[8] [Agerby (1889–1942) was an organist, composer and administrator, and had been President of the Association of Young Musicians since 1929.]

their mark on Danish musical life had gathered there for the first time, ardently discussing the newest things in music and, of course, the evening's compositions.

Now one mustn't think that there was talk of a 'praisers' club', a society for mutual uncritical admiration. No, some frank comments could be made and some strong criticism handed out, which nevertheless always originated in sympathy and understanding; but on the other hand, there was no hesitation when it was a matter of recognising something that was well written or that seemed to contain possibilities for the future. My trio got its share of praise and criticism, and that took on some significance, especially as the comments were made at the beginning of the party. At some point a little later in the night, the violinist Niels Borre presented to me, with great ceremony, a medal in the form of an old leather button, in special recognition 'of my contribution'. I accepted it with deep thanks, and everything was just fine, but it was better still that there was to be more than just buttons and discussion.

Emil Telmányi,[9] who also conducted at that time, spoke to me and said he had seen a concerto for orchestra that I had recently written. Well, after hearing the trio, he was interested in performing it (the concerto) in a concert a few months later – did I mind? I certainly didn't, and in April 1933 my first orchestral work was performed by Telmányi at the Danish Concert Society.[10] But this performance, which was to be my first real appearance in Danish music, actually lies beyond the domain of the debut. At that point one had already learned from experience and had begun to climb up the mountain towards the destination, which nevertheless kept fading from sight and still fades behind yet new mountaintops. However, that is not what one was thinking that innocent evening, when one had not read the papers but had already conquered the world.

[9] Born in Hungary in 1892, Telmányi has lived in Denmark since 1919. Between the Wars he gained an international reputation as a violinist and conductor. As a violinist he had a close association with the music of Carl Nielsen (whose son-in-law he was) and with the music of the Baroque.

[10] [The work, performed on 3 April 1933, was the Concerto for Orchestra, M. 41, of 1931.]

HUMAN RESPONSIBILITY
AND ARTISTIC FREEDOM

I am absolutely certain that no one can ever speak completely truthfully when trying to tell about how he became a composer. Everything depends on memory, and memory is not entirely reliable. *Some* things are remembered, the broad outlines, certain major explosions, and a great many unsorted and random details; but important things undoubtedly are forgotten – perhaps because they are of no value in the circumstances of the moment and thus are pushed so far back in the brain that thinking cannot bring them out.

But let me try a very broad outline.

We were seven children, and our interest in artistic matters was encouraged in the home, where the arts were pursued in moderation, both collectively and individually. However, we were certainly not encouraged to become artists, and it was against our parents' wishes that a few of us tried to advance along that thorny path.

I myself was affected early by all the muses, by everything that could be termed artistic. And I knew already as a boy (but for good reasons told no one) that I could exist only in a world where artistic concerns were dominant, and that I would have to be active within this world. By contrast, the choice of means and medium was more subordinate for me, in the sense that until a certain point, I pursued with equal enthusiasm word, tone, thought, form and colour. But a choice among the arts became quite unavoidable, and various events brought it about that music won the struggle. In this branch of the arts my technical abilities and theoretical knowledge were not extensive, and accordingly the road became particularly rough and long.

The end of the road has not been reached yet, as there are constantly new things to learn. For that matter, my path of development can be drawn as a rather common and well-known curve.

When quite young the artist was conservative and conformist, respectful of conventions and tradition. Later he became radical and conformist, with a corresponding disrespect for everything conventional. He lived in a little world of relative aggression and narrow-mindedness (apparently a biological necessity), but a world, fortunately, whose narrow boundaries were soon broken through: gradually he ran into problems and demands of various sorts; sometimes they came from within, sometimes from without, but they had a tendency to pile up in an alarming manner. He grew less rigid in his opinions, less interested in experiments and artistic debates. He immersed himself in work, found his means of expression, and developed as best he could.

In other words, he calmed down.

Now he could be content and remain in a state of taking pleasure in his work and of isolated peace: after all, he had managed to express himself under certain circumstances, and there *were* other concerns besides art in the world.

There are, to be sure, other concerns besides art in this world. But an artist has only his own mind, and if it cannot be content and stay satisfied, nothing can be done about it. He is compelled to move on, to set aside the results in hand, to look deeper and farther. He goes through a constant alternation between periods of calm, when works are created and results are obtained, and periods of disruption, when some things are abandoned and new problems are taken up, new lessons are learned. And gradually he finds that after all he does not have only his own mind, but that he is compelled to carry experiences from as far back as the childhood of humanity, a burden that gets heavier and heavier with the years. He sees that he is a small link in constant changes around the same centre, that he himself changes and so must also bring about change. Thus the meaningful, the artistically significant always lies ahead. And that is where it still lies for me.

Every new thing an artist works on pushes all the previous things out of his consciousness. He completely loses interest in anything but what he is shaping at that very time; that alone is essential, that alone is his whole world, a cosmos that forms around him.

How the creative process works is difficult or impossible to describe. The artist himself cannot be inside the process and at the same time observe it. It will again depend on a memory that is just as remote and unreliable whether it is five minutes or five months since the process was in action.

The impulse for a work may come from within or from without. It may be a commission, a few lines in a book, some tones that suddenly become meaningful, a rhythm, a chance remark – it may be nearly anything. Such sources of inspiration work indirectly and are beyond control. An artist can never fully know anything about how he works, and he is, in addition, not very interested; for the most crucial thing of all is that his mind has begun to stir and that something or other that has long been going on in his mind now suddenly becomes conscious. This 'something or other' is in the beginning almost always like a kind of foggy space, an unclear sensation of a totality, which one has for a short or a long time while it slowly takes shape. Only after consciousness steps in can the manual work begin.

Accordingly, a composer can also never know how much his personal feelings and dispositions are significant for what he writes. At most he may remember that there often seems to be a certain clash between attitude of mind and what the task involves and insists on involving.

A composer can be sad at heart and write spirited music, angry and write gentle music, just as it can, of course, be the other way around. Whether his music is subjective or objective, he himself does not know, but he does know that, if it is to be good, he must give everything he has, completely and without reservation. The work has its own particular laws when it first gets going, and if he tries defiantly to follow his own head he will soon be taught something else. A good number of erasers wears down if he tries to evade the issue, because he is incessantly forced back to the work and can satisfy himself only when it has become wholly 'itself', has become so right that he is then in a position to write it.

Now, of course, it is not a question of a conflict between the person and the given work (even if it is felt as such), but of an endless contest between intellect and awareness on one side and intuition about the completed work on the other.

It is my experience that intuition, emotion, intellect and craft must have a certain mutually balanced relationship, if what one writes is to be even moderately good. There can be more or less tension between these elements, but if one of them becomes too dominating, the result will very easily become a monstrosity, a detached part of the whole. Perhaps an interesting but lifeless object of contemplation, a shapeless intuition, a chaos of emotion, or a superficial technical virtuosity.

This experience is, so far as I understand, with certain modifications and variations, fairly common for composers of all times; anyhow, I cannot get around it without deluding myself or betraying what I write.

From this it follows that I am bound by a tradition (if it may be called such here), namely, that which limits art to being expression for those conditions and possibilities that the human being can grasp. That sounds self-evident and even ought to be so; but at times many confuse cause and effect by transferring the concept of tradition to the means – which can create some confusion and is damaging to a clear view of art and its functions.

As a composer I must have the feeling of being completely free regarding the employment of means. I must have the right not to be tied down by the established way, to reject what I have no use for and to choose that which I may deem necessary for the case at hand. The responsibility is inevitably mine, and it is above all a responsibility for the work, its nature and character.

Only in this two-fold situation of human responsibility and artistic freedom can I work and develop my music.

My interest in the results of artistic endeavours is not deep and is essentially limited to learning the errors I might have made. For what one has previously written will very readily act as a constriction of one's artistic freedom and create a personal tradition that will stiffen to the point of mannerism and prevent new views if it becomes wholly conscious.

As long as a composer is really able to change and develop, his music must also change. Everything depends of course on the particular foundation, on the crucial limitations that lie in the purely human, in the composer's own character, ability and creative power.

SELECT BIBLIOGRAPHY
OF ITEMS IN ENGLISH
BY AND ON
VAGN HOLMBOE

In the listing below, the third-last item is a book; the others are articles. Some require some musical background on the part of the reader, but most do not.

JÜRGEN BALZER, 'Vagn Holmboe', *Catalogue of Danish Music on Records*, European HMV-Columbia, Copenhagen, 1947.
——, 'Vagn Holmboe – Portrait of a Composer', *Musical Denmark*, No. 21, pp. 4–7.

GRAHAM CARRITT, 'Vagn Holmboe', *Anglo Dania*, Vol. 27, No. 5, November 1958, pp. 26–28 (virtually the same as the following).
——, 'Vagn Holmboe', *Monthly Musical Record*, Vol. 88, No. 986, March–April 1958, pp. 58–63.
——, 'Vagn Holmboe: a Modern Danish Composer', *The Listener*, Vol. 59, No. 1502, 9 January 1958, p. 81.

IAN FINNEY, 'Quartet Composer at Work: Vagn Holmboe', *Tempo*, No. 171, December 1989, pp. 12–17.

VAGN HOLMBOE, 'On Form and Metamorphosis', in John Beckwith and Udo Kasemets (eds.), *The Modern Composer and his World*, University of Toronto Press, Toronto, 1961, pp. 134–40.

VAGN KAPPEL, *Contemporary Danish Composers*, The Danish Institute, Copenhagen, 1967, pp. 68–71.

ROBERT LAYTON, 'Vagn Holmboe', in Stanley Sadie (ed.), *The New Grove Dictionary of Music and Musicians*, Vol. 8, Macmillan, London, 1980, pp. 653–55.
——, 'Vagn Holmboe and the later Scandinavians', in Robert Simpson (ed.), *The Symphony*, Vol. 2, Penguin, Harmondsworth, 1967, pp. 230–42.

———, 'Vagn Holmboe and the Quartet', *The Musical Times*, Vol. 110, No. 1522, December 1969, pp. 1232–34.

ANDREW McCREDIE, 'Twentieth-century Danish Music', *Canon*, Vol. 13, Nos. 7/8, March/April 1960, pp. 212–16.

———, 'Vagn Holmboe – a Versatile Nestor of Contemporary Danish Music', *The Chesterian*, Vol. 36, No. 208, Autumn 1961, pp. 34–41.

POUL NIELSEN, 'Some Comments on Vagn Holmboe's Idea of Metamorphosis', *Dansk aarbog for musikforskning*, VI, 1968–72, pp. 159–69.

PAUL RAPOPORT, *Vagn Holmboe: a Catalogue of his Music, Discography, Bibliography, Essays*, 2nd edn., Edition Wilhelm Hansen, Copenhagen, 1979.

———, 'Vagn Holmboe and his Symphony No. 7', in *Opus Est: Six Composers from Northern Europe*, Kahn and Averill, London, 1978/Taplinger, New York, 1979, pp. 49–74, 194, 199.

NILS SCHIØRRING, 'Vagn Holmboe – a Danish Composer', *Musical Denmark*, No. 5, June 1954, pp. 1–2.

BO WALLNER, 'Scandinavian Music after the Second World War', in Paul Henry Lang and Nathan Broder (eds.), *Contemporary Music in Europe*, W. W. Norton, New York, 1968, pp. 111–43.

Index

Vagn Holmboe